And they brought unto him also infants, that he would touch them: but when his disciples saw it, they rebuked them.

But Jesus called them unto him, and said, Suffer little children to come unto me, and forbid them not: for of such is the kingdom of God.

Verily I say unto you, Whosoever shall not receive the kingdom of God as a little child shall in no wise enter therein.

(Luke 18:15–17)

# THE FAMILY

# AND

# THE NATION

## BIBLICAL CHILDHOOD

BY ROSALIE J. SLATER

INTRODUCTION BY CAROLE G. ADAMS

FOUNDATION FOR AMERICAN CHRISTIAN EDUCATION

SAN FRANCISCO, CALIFORNIA

ANNO DOMINI 2002

*The Family and the Nation—Biblical Childhood*
by Rosalie J. Slater

Copyright December 25, 2002; 2012 by the
Foundation for American Christian Education

Published by the
Foundation for American Christian Education

ISBN 978-0-912498-27-0

BOOKS BY ROSALIE J. SLATER

*Teaching and Learning America's Christian History:*
*The Principle Approach;*

*Rudiments of America's Christian History and Government:*
*Student Handbook* (with Verna M. Hall);

*The Bible and the Constitution of the United States of America*
(with Verna M. Hall);

*A Family Program for Reading Aloud;*

*The Noah Plan Literature Curriculum Guide*

Free Catalogue & Ordering:

F. A. C. E., PO BOX 9588

CHESAPEAKE, VIRGINIA 23321

800-352-FACE • www.face.net

DESIGN & GRAPHICS:
*Desta Garrett*

COVER PICTURE:

*The Beloved Son*
Cicely Mary Barker, Artist
Girls Friendly Society, London
By Permission

DEDICATION

To Carole Adams, founder and head of StoneBridge School,

and to the families for whom it was established;

and to Tom and Christi Moorman, who brought

their six children from Texas to Virginia to attend:

Muffin, Amelita, Tom, John, Zachery, and Moses

# CONTENTS

# LET OUR YOUTH BE INSTRUCTED  117

# ILLUSTRATIONS

# INTRODUCTION

## by Carole G. Adams

The Spirit of God through Christ issues loving but compelling invitations. Jesus *invited* his followers to join the greatest adventure in human history. He invited his hearers to have ears to hear and eyes to see. He issued invitations to the Kingdom of Heaven, to His Father's mansion, and to the banqueting table of the Lamb. There was no coercion, no force, no arm-twisting, just open hands, open arms, and open heart—an open invitation.

> Invite, v. [L. *invito*; to bid] 1. To ask to do some act or to go to some place; to request the company of a person; as, to invite one to dine or sup; to invite friends to a wedding; to invite company to an entertainment; to invite one to an excursion in the country. 2. To allure; to draw to; to tempt to come; to induce by pleasure or hope.

Just so, Rosalie June Slater's work *The Family and the Nation* is a beautifully illustrated, lovingly phrased invitation to Christian families today, begging their attention to consider and ponder *Biblical Childhood*. It is a conclusive compilation of the *vox dei*, the voice of God concerning the Biblical norm for child growth and development. This book is *not* the latest self-help guide for families from current Christian psychology's wisdom. It is *not* the law and the commandment. It *is* the *sola scriptura* method and standard for child-rearing. And it *is* delivered through the eloquence and literary excellence of the greatest Christian commentators and writers.

The spirit of this book lures the reader to watch and see, in the lives of five great Biblical characters, God's heart for childhood. Moses, Samuel, David, John, and Jesus—directly from the Old Testament and New Testament accounts—are on stage. The playwrights—Hannah More, Charles John Ellicott, Arthur Pink, James Stalker, Alfred Edersheim, Josephus, and Matthew Henry—are all great commentators and scholars of reformed Christianity. Miss Slater has woven their vivid and profound accounts of Biblical childhood into a masterwork for the inspiration of today's moms and dads who long to practice Biblical parenting.

The reader should consider this book a plea to square our standards of child rearing with the standards of Jesus. Never has this topic, *The Family and the Nation: Biblical Childhood*, been more vital to life in America. Nearly everyone in America now agrees that family disintegration is a prime cause of much of our contemporary social malaise. The resulting arguments of cause and effect, who to blame, how to solve our problems suffer from a lack of 'true' truth or principle. *The Family and the Nation: Biblical Childhood* proposes a return to the Bible as the norm of norms—the normative expression of a rightly ordered family for blessing.

The book is richly illustrated from the masters: Benjamin West, Murillo, Louis de Boulogne, Raphael, N. C. Wyeth, Tissot, and others. It is true to its mission of offering the Biblical account as model for study and application. The depth and breadth of the writers' insight is startlingly fresh and affirming, causing the reader new respect and boundless appreciation for the Bible itself. In discussing "Christ's Literary Style" in chapter two, James Stalker says,

> "Such was the form of the teaching of Jesus. It consisted of numerous sayings, everyone of which contained the greatest possible amount of truth in the smallest possible compass, and was expressed in language so concise and pointed as to stick in the memory like an arrow. . . ."

So it is with the Bible generally. And so it is with this book. The stories themselves teach the greatest possible amount of truth in the smallest possible compass, and express it in language so concise and pointed as to stick in the memory like an arrow.

The Foundation for American Christian Education presents this volume, first in a series of three of Rosalie Slater's works, inviting Christian parents, grandparents, teachers, and families to love and admire the Word of God while realizing its powerful voice in the matters of childhood.

# Citation Sources & Key to Abbreviations

Abbreviations as
used in Citations

Drinkwater, John, ed. *The Outline of Literature*, Vol. I–II.
    London: George Newnes Limited, 1924.           Drinkwater, Vol. _

Edersheim, Alfred *Bible History Old Testament*. Grand Rapids:
    William B. Eerdmans, 1972.           Edersheim, *O.T.*
\_\_\_\_ *The Life and Times of Jesus the Messiah*. Peabody, MA:
    Hendrickson Publishers; Complete one volume edition, 1993.    Edersheim, *Messiah*
\_\_\_\_ *Sketches of Jewish Social Life in the Days of Christ.*
    Grand Rapids: William B. Eerdmans, 1972.    Edersheim, *Sketches*
\_\_\_\_ *The Temple: Its Ministry and Services.* Grand Rapids, MI:
    William B. Eerdmans, 1976.    Edersheim, *Temple*

Ellicott, Charles John, D.D. *An Old Testament Commentary for English*
    *Readers,* Vols. I–V. London: Cassell & Company Limited, 1884.    Ellicott, *O.T.*, Vol. _
\_\_\_\_ *A New Testament Commentary for English Readers,* Vols. I–III,
    London: Cassell , Petter, Galpin & Co., 1883.    Ellicott, *N.T.*, Vol. _

Halsey, LeRoy Jones *The Literary Attractions of the Bible; or A Plea for the*
    *Word of God, Considered as a Classic,* 3rd Edition. New York:
    Charles Scribner & Co., 1866.    Halsey

Henry, Matthew *Commentary on the Whole Bible,* Vols. I–VI.
    New York: Fleming H. Revell Company.    Henry, Vol. _

Josephus, Flavius *The Works of Flavius Josephus* (37?–100), 1837    Josephus

More, Hannah *Sacred Dramas Chiefly Intended for Young Persons: Subjects Taken*
    *from the Bible,* "Moses in the Bulrushes." Newark: W. Tuttle & Co., 1806.    More

Pink, Arthur W. *Gleanings in Genesis.* Chicago: Moody Press, 1922, 1950.    Pink, *Genesis*
\_\_\_\_ *Gleanings in Exodus.* Chicago: Moody Press, 1971.    Pink, *Exodus*
\_\_\_\_ *The Life of David,* 2 volumes in one. Swengel, PA: Reiner Publications, 1974.    Pink, *David*

Ryken, Leland *The Literature of the Bible.* Grand Rapids, MI: Zondervan
    Publishing House, 1974.    Ryken

Stalker, Rev. James, D.D. *The Life of Jesus Christ.* American Tract Society,
    Revised Edition Fleming H. Revell Company, 1891.    Stalker

Smith, Sir William and Rev. J. M. Fuller, Editors. *Dictionary of the Bible*
    *Comprising Its Antiquities, Biography, Geography, and Natural*
    *History.* London: John Murray, 1893.    Smith

# F.A.C.E. Resources & Citations

Abbreviations as
used in Citations

Hall, Verna M. *The Christian History of the American Revolution:
Consider and Ponder*, 1975.

*Consider & Ponder*

Hall, Verna M. *The Christian History of the Constitution of the United States
of America*, Vol. I: *Christian Self-Government*, 1960, and
Vol. II: *Christian Self-Government with Union*, 1962.

CHOC
SGWU

Johnston, Annie Fellows *Joel: A Boy of Galilee*, (written 1898), 1992.

Slater, Rosalie J. *The Family and the Nation: Biblical Childhood*, 2002.

Slater, *Biblical Childhood*

Slater, Rosalie J. *The Noah Plan Bible Curriculum Guide* (under production)

Slater, Rosalie J. *The Noah Plan Literature Curriculum Guide*, 1997.

Slater, *Literature*

Slater, Rosalie J. *Teaching and Learning America's Christian History:
The Principle Approach*, 1965.

*T & L*

Webster, Noah *The American Dictionary of the English Language*
(Facsimile 1828 Edition), 1967.

Webster, *Dictionary*

# The Family
## and
# The Nation


## Moses

Moses Coming Down from Mount Sinai
by Gustave Doré

# THE FAMILY AND THE NATION

Babyhood and the fate of a nation is painted in rich, indelible colors of feeling and character in the opening chapter of the book of Exodus. In fact, this is the record of the most significant babyhood in the Old Testament. Such a few words to describe an incredible series of events as far as history is concerned! Ten verses describe this babyhood. Only the events which follow help us deduce the invisible, internal factors which shaped the future. As we turn to the first chapter of *Exodus* we learn of the death of Joseph *"and all his brethren, and all that generation."* With the new generation arose up *"a new king over Egypt, which knew not Joseph."* As Flavius Josephus (37?–100) the learned Jewish historian, wrote:

"... Joseph also died when he had lived a hundred and ten years; having been a man of admirable virtue, and conducting all his affairs by the rules of reason; and used his authority with moderation, which was the cause of his so great felicity among the Egyptians, even when he came from another country, ..." (Josephus, page 74)

The Egyptians had "... forgotten the benefits they had received from Joseph...." (Josephus, page 75) There was a spiritual decline in the Egyptians. They became a pleasure-oriented people, jealous of the children of Israel who *"were, fruitful, and increased abundantly, and multiplied, and waxed exceeding mighty; and the land was filled with them."*

We know of this period of four hundred years of bondage and of the afflictions endured by the children of Israel. Yet, even at this darkest moment of their history, God was preparing a Deliverer. Josephus records that the Egyptians were forewarned of his arrival.

"... One of those sacred scribes, ... who are very sagacious in foretelling future events truly, told the king, that about this time there would be a child born to the Israelites, who if he were reared, would bring the Egyptian dominion low, and would raise the Israelites; that he would excel all men in virtue, and obtain a glory that would be remembered through all ages...." (Josephus, page 75)

This prophecy caused the new King of Egypt, the Pharaoh, to decree the death of all male children born to the Israelites. Thus the King went after the most effective means of the genocide of the children of Israel —the slaughter of their sons, even as another king resorted to the same evil tactic some 1500 years later, fearing the birth of the Messiah.

The second Book of Moses indicates that the King spoke directly to midwives that they might police the labours of the Hebrew women.

*"And the king of Egypt spake to the Hebrew midwives, of which the name of the one was Shiphrah, and the name of the other Puah: And he said, When ye do the office of a midwife to the Hebrew women, and see them upon the stools; if it be a son, then ye shall kill him: but if it be a daughter, then she shall live."* (Exodus 1:15–16)

Bible scholars argue whether these two midwives were not Hebrew women, but rather Egyptian. Yet the Semitic character of their names suggest that they were members of the peculiar people. Shiphrah means "beautiful." Puah means "one who cries out." (Ellicott, *O.T.*, Vol. I, page 194) Scripture also tells us: *"But the midwives feared God, and did not as the king of Egypt commanded them, but saved the men children alive."*

There is no record that any Egyptian at this time knew or feared God—and this is the first indication among the Hebrews that God was giving courage to honor what would become one of His most sacred commandments—*"Thou shalt not kill."* That the midwives who refused to kill the Hebrew children were under God's protection we know for the Word tells us:

*"Therefore God dealt well with the midwives: and the people multiplied and waxed very mighty. And it came to pass, because the midwives feared God, that he made them houses."* As one Bible commentator writes: "God rewarded those who had showed tenderness to young children, by giving them children of their own, who grew up, and became in their turn fathers and mothers of families." (Ellicott, *O.T.*, Vol. I, page 194)

Thus at the very time when Moses was to be born, Pharaoh had charged all his people, saying *"Every son that is born ye shall cast into the river, and every daughter ye shall save alive."* (Exodus 1:22)

Nothing can be too hard for the purposes of God. The child whom the sacred scribes of Egypt foretold was also foretold to the Lord's people. Josephus writes:

"A man whose name was Amram, one of the nobler sort of the Hebrews, was afraid for his whole nation, lest it should fail, by the want of young men to be brought up hereafter, and was very uneasy at it, his wife being then with child, and he knew not what to do. Hereupon he betook himself to prayer to God; and entreated him to have compassion on those men who had nowise transgressed the laws of his worship, and to afford them deliverance from the miseries they at that time endured, and to render abortive their enemies' hopes of the destruction of their nation.

". . . Accordingly God had mercy on him, and was moved by his supplication. He stood by him in his sleep, and exhorted him not to despair of his future favours. He said further, that he did not forget their piety towards him, and would always reward them for it, as he had formerly granted his favour to their forefathers, and made them increase from a few to so great a multitude. . . .

". . . Know therefore that I shall provide for you all in common what is for your good, and particularly for thyself what shall make thee famous; for that child, out of dread of whose nativity the Egyptians have doomed the Israelite children to destruction, shall be this child of thine, and shall be concealed from those who watch to destroy him: and when he is brought up in a surprising way, he shall deliver the Hebrew nation from the distress they are under from the Egyptians. His memory shall be famous while the world lasts; and this not only among the Hebrews, but foreigners also: . . ." (Josephus, page 75)

The Apostle Paul declares in the Book of Hebrews the motivating force of Moses parents, Amram and Jochebed:

*"By faith Moses, when he was born, was hid three months of his parents, because they saw he was a proper child; and they were not afraid of the king's commandment."* (Hebrews 11:23)

In his commentary on this passage, Dr. Arthur Pink reminds us: "Faith 'cometh by *hearing*' Romans 10:17. The parents of Moses, must, therefore, have received a direct communication from God, informing them of what should happen and instructing them what to do. And they believed what God had told

4

FLAVIUS JOSEPHUS,

them and acted accordingly." (Pink, *Exodus,* page 17)

Amram and Jochebed overcame their fear of the king and trusted in the protection of God for preserving the life of their child. In effect, they acted against the civil authorities of their time and were obedient to the directions given to them by God, even as the midwives. *"Then Peter and the other apostles answered and said, We ought to obey God rather than men."* (Acts 5:29)

Two children had already been born to Amram and Jochebed. They were Aaron and Miriam. Aaron was old enough to have escaped the cruel edict of the king in regard to male Hebrew children. When Moses was born, Jochebed's feelings struggled until her faith prevailed. *"He was a goodly child, she hid him three months."* (Exodus 2:2)

The facts of Moses' birth and preservation are well known to us through our study of Scripture. But let us now introduce the "handmaid" of literature to extend our appreciation and contemplation of this wondrous event and its significance for the family. In the eighteenth century one of the most widely read authors in both England and America was Hannah More (1745–1833). Miss More was an English evangelical, active both in academic and Sunday school education. As a writer she dealt with the subjects of the day in verse, ballad, drama, and treatise. Her essays on practical piety, female education, and the character formation of the royal princess fascinate us. But most pertinent to our own education of youth are Hannah More's *Sacred Dramas* published first in 1782 and migrating across the ocean to appear in print in America by the 1800s.

SACRED DRAMAS,
Chiefly Intended for
YOUNG PERSONS
Subjects Taken from the Bible
To Which Are Added,
REFLECTIONS OF KING HEZEKIAH;
SENSIBILITY, a Poem;
and
SEARCH AFTER HAPPINESS

by Hannah More

"All the books of the BIBLE are either the most admirable
and most exalted pieces of poetry, or are the best materials
in the world for it." (Cowley)

Newark; Printed by W. Tuttle & Co.
1806

The titles of the SACRED DRAMAS
by Miss More
are as follows:
MOSES IN THE BULRUSHES
DAVID AND GOLIATH
BELSHAZZAR
DANIEL

Miss More has this to say about her *Sacred Dramas*:

"In the construction of them, I have seldom ventured to introduce any persons of my own creation: still less did I imagine myself at liberty to invent circumstances. I reflected with awe, *that the place whereon I stood was holy ground*. All the latitude I permitted myself, was to make such persons as I selected, act under such circumstances as I found, and express such sentiments, as, in my humble judgment, appeared not unnatural to their situations. Some of the speeches are so long as to retard the action; for I rather aspired after Moral Instruction, than the purity of Dramatic Composition."

We have interwoven Hannah More's Sacred Drama *Moses in the Bulrushes* with some of the commentary by Bible teachers. We hope that this may introduce the use of literature into our study of history – for all history, whether called sacred or secular, is under the Sovereignty of God.

6

MOSES IN THE BULRUSHES
A Sacred Drama

I will assert eternal Providence,
And justify the way of God to man.
(Milton, *Paradise Lost*)

Persons of the Drama

HEBREW WOMEN
*Jochebed*, mother of Moses
*Miriam*, his sister

EGYPTIANS
*The Princess*, King Pharaoh's daughter
*Melita*, and other attendants

SCENE—On the banks of the Nile.

This subject is taken from the Second Chapter of the Book of Exodus.

PART ONE
In the House of Moses
Jochebed, Miriam

JOCHEBED
WHY was my pray'r accepted? why did Heav'n
In anger hear me, when I ask'd a son?
Ye dames of Egypt! happy, happy mothers!
No tyrant robs you of your fondest hopes;
You are not doom'd to see the babes you bore,
The babes you nurture, bleed before your eyes!
You taste the transports of maternal love,
And never know its anguish! happy mothers!
How diff'rent is the lot of thy sad daughters,
O wretched Israel! Was it then for this,
Was it for this the righteous arm of GOD
Rescued his chosen people from the jaws
Of cruel want, by pious Joseph's care?
Joseph! th'elected instrument of Heav'n,
Decreed to save illustrious Abraham's race,
What time the famine rag'd in Canaan's land.
Israel, who then was spar'd, must perish now!
　　Oh thou mysterious Power! who has involv'd
Thy wise decrees in darkness, to perplex
The pride of human wisdom, to confound

The daring scrutiny, and prove the faith
Of thy presuming creatures! clear this doubt;
Teach me to trace this maze of Providence;
Why save the fathers, if the sons must perish?

MIRIAM
    Ah me, my mother! whence these floods of grief?

JOCHEBED
    My son! my son! I cannot speak the rest.
Ye who have sons can only know my fondness!
Ye who have lost them, or who fear to lose,
Can only know my pangs! none else can guess them.
A mother's sorrows cannot be conceiv'd,
But by a mother—Wherefore am I one?

MIRIAM
    With many prayers thou didst request this son,
And Heav'n has granted him.

JOCHEBED
                                        O sad estate
Of human wretchedness! so weak is man,
So ignorant and blind, that did not GOD
Sometimes withhold in mercy what we ask,
We should be ruin'd at our own request.
    Too well thou know'st, my child, the stern decree
Of Egypt's cruel king, hard-hearted Pharaoh;
"That ev'ry male of Hebrew mother born,
"Must die." Oh! do I live to tell it thee?
Must die a bloody death! My child, my son,
My youngest born, my darling must be slain!

MIRIAM
    The helpless innocent! and must he die?

JOCHEBED
    No: if a mother's tears, a mother's prayers,
A mother's fond precautions can prevail,
He shall not die. I have a thought, my Miriam!
And sure the God of mercies, who inspir'd,

Will bless the secret purpose of my soul,
To save his precious life.

MIRIAM

     Hop'st thou that Pharaoh—

JOCHEBED

 I have no hope in Pharaoh, much in GOD;
Much in the *Rock of Ages*.

MIRIAM

     Think, O think,
What perils thou already has incurr'd;
And shun the greater, which may yet remain.
Three months, three dang'rous months thou hast preserv'd
Thy infant's life, and in thy house conceal'd him!
Should Pharaoh know!

JOCHEBED

     Oh! let the tyrant know,
And feel what he inflicts! Yes, hear me, Heav'n!
Send the right aiming thunderbolts—— But hush,
My impious murmurs! Is it not thy will,
Thou infinite in mercy? Thou permitt'st
This seeming evil for some latent good.
Yes, I will laud thy grace, and bless thy goodness
For what I have, and not arraign thy wisdom
For what I fear to lose. O, I will bless thee,
That Aaron will be spar'd! that my first born
Lives safe and undisturb'd! that he was given me
Before this impious persecution rag'd!

MIRIAM

 And yet who knows but the fell tyrant's rage
May reach *his* precious life?

JOCHEBED

     I fear for him,
For thee, for all. A doating parent lives
In many lives; thro' many a nerve she feels;
From child to child the quick affections spread,
For ever wand'ring, yet for ever fix'd.

Nor does division weaken, nor the force
Of constant operation e'er exhaust
Parental love. All other passions change
With changing circumstances; rise or fall,
Dependent on their object; claim returns;
Live on reciprocation, and expire
Unfed by hope. A mother's fondness reigns
Without a rival and without an end.

MIRIAM
    But say what Heav'n inspires to save thy son?

JOCHEBED
    Since the dear fatal morn which gave him birth,
I have revolv'd in my distracted mind
Each mean to save his life; and many a thought,
Which fondness prompted, prudence has oppos'd
As perilous and rash. With these poor hands
I've fram'd a little ark of slender reeds;
With pitch and slime I have secur'd the sides:
In this frail cradle I intend to lay
My little helpless infant, and expose him
Upon the banks of Nile.

MIRIAM
                  'Tis full of danger.

JOCHEBED
    'Tis danger to expose, and death to keep him.

MIRIAM
    Yet, Oh! reflect. Should the fierce crocodile,
The native and the tyrant of the Nile,
Seize the defenceless infant!

JOCHEBED
               Oh, forbear!
Spare my fond heart. Yet not the crocodile,
Nor all the deadly monsters of the deep,
To me are half so terrible as PHARAOH,
That heathen king, that royal murderer!

MIRIAM

   Should he escape (which yet I dare not hope)
Each sea-born monster, yet the winds and waves
He cannot 'scape.

JOCHEBED

               Know, GOD is ev'rywhere;
Not to one narrow, partial spot confin'd;
No, not to chosen ISRAEL: He extends
Thro' all the vast infinitude of space.
At his command the furious tempests rise,
The blasting of the breath of his displeasure:
He tells the world of waters when to roar;
And at his bidding, winds and seas are calm.
In HIM, not in an arm of flesh, I trust;
In HIM, whose promise never yet has fail'd,
I place my confidence.

MIRIAM

             What must I do?
Command thy daughter, for thy words have wak'd
An holy boldness in my youthful breast.

JOCHEBED

   Go then, my MIRIAM! go, and take the infant.
Buried in harmless slumbers there he lies:
Let me not see him—spare my heart that pang.
Yet sure one little look may be indulg'd,
One kiss—perhaps the last. No more my soul!
That fondness would be fatal—I should keep him.
I could not doom to death the babe I clasp'd.
Did ever mother kill her sleeping boy?
I dare not hazard it—The task be thine.
Oh! do not wake my child; remove him softly;
And gently lay him on the river's brink.

MIRIAM

   Did those magicians whom the sons of Egypt
Consult, and think all-potent, join their skill,
And was it great as Egypt's sons believe;
Yet all their secret wizard arts combin'd
To save this little ark of Bulrushes,

Thus fearfully expos'd could not effect it.
Their spells, their incantations, and dire charms
Could not preserve it.

JOCHEBED
                    Know, this ark is charm'd
With spells, which impious Egypt never knew:
With invocations to the living GOD
I twisted every slender reed together,
And with a prayer did every osier weave.

MIRIAM
    I go.

JOCHEBED
            Yet e'er thou goest observe me well,
When thou hast laid him in his watry bed,
O leave him not, but at a distance wait,
And mark what Heav'n's high will determines for him.
Lay him among the flags on yonder beach,
Just where the royal gardens meet the Nile.
I dare not follow him, Suspicion's eye
Would note my wild demeanor; MIRIAM, yes,
The mother's fondness would betray the child.
Farewell! GOD of my fathers, Oh protect him!

PART TWO

SCENE, on the banks of the Nile.

*Enter Miriam, after having deposed the child.*

MIRIAM
YES, I have laid him in his watry bed,
His watry grave, I fear! —I tremble still;
It was a cruel task—still I must weep!
But ah! my mother, who shall soothe thy griefs?
The flags and sea-weeds will awhile sustain
Their precious load, but it must sink ere long!
Sweet babe, farewell! Yet think not I will leave thee;
No, I will watch thee, til the greedy waves
Devour thy little bark: I'll sit me down,

12

And sing to thee, sweet babe! Thou canst not hear;
But 'twill amuse me while I watch they fate.

*She sits down on a bank, and sings.*

### SONG

I
    THOU, who canst make the feeble strong,
    O GOD of Israel, hear my song!
Not mine such notes as Egypt's daughters raise;
'Tis thee, O GOD of Hosts, I strive to please.

II
    Ye winds the servants of the LORD,
    Ye waves obedient to this word,
O spare the babe committed to your trust;
And Israel shall confess the LORD is just!

III
    Tho' doom'd to find an early grave,
    This helpless infant thou canst save;
And he, whose death's decreed by Pharaoh's hand,
May rise a prophet to redeem the land.

*She rises and looks out.*

    Who moves this way? of royal port she seems;
Perhaps sent hither by the hand of Heav'n,
To prop the falling house of Levi— Soft;
I'll listen unperceiv'd these trees will hide me.

*She stands behind.*

*Enter the Princess of Egypt, attended by a train of Ladies.*

PRINCESS
    No farther, virgins; here I mean to rest,
To taste the pleasant coolness of the breeze;
Perhaps to bathe in this translucent stream.
Did not our holy law* enjoin th' ablution
Frequent and regular; it still were needful,

---

* The ancient Egyptians used to wash their bodies four
times every twenty-four hours.

To mitigate the fervors of our clime.
MELITA, stay—the rest at distance wait.
*They all go out, except one.*

*The Princess looks out.*
    Sure, or I much mistake, or I perceive,
Upon the sedgy margin of the Nile
A chest; entangled in the reeds it seems;
Discerns't thou aught?

MELITA
                Something, but what I know not.

PRINCESS
    Go, and examine what this sight may mean.
*Exit maid.*

MIRIAM *(behind)*
    O, blest beyond my hopes! he is discover'd;
My brother will be sav'd! who is this stranger?
Ah! 'tis the Princess, cruel Pharaoh's daughter.
If she resemble her inhuman sire,
She must be cruel too; yet fame reports her
Most merciful and mild: —I'll mark th' event,
And pray that Heav'n may prompt her to preserve him.

*Re-enter Melita.*

PRINCESS
    Hast thou discover'd what the vessel is?

MELITA
    Oh, Princess, I have seen the strangest sight!
Within the vessel lies a sleeping babe,
A fairer infant have I never seen!

PRINCESS
    Who knows, but some unhappy Hebrew woman
Has thus expos'd her infant, to evade
The stern decree of my too cruel sire?
Unhappy mothers! oft my heart has bled
In secret anguish o'er your slaughter'd sons.

MELITA
Should this be one, my Princess knows the danger.

PRINCESS
No danger should deter from acts of mercy.

MIRIAM *(behind)*
A thousand blessings on her princely head!

PRINCESS
Too much the sons of Jacob have endur'd
From royal Pharaoh's unrelenting hate;
Too much our house has crush'd their alien race.
Is't not enough that cruel task-masters
Grind them by hard oppression and stern bondage?
Is't not enough, my father owes his greatness,
His palaces, his fanes* magnificent;
Those structures which the world with wonder views,
To the hard toils of much insulted Israel?
To them his growing cities owe their splendor,
Their labours built fair Ramses and Pythom;
And now, at length, his still increasing rage
To iron bondage adds the guilt of murder.
And shall this little helpless infant perish?
Forbid it, justice; and forbid it, Heav'n!

MELITA
I know thy royal father fears the strength
Of this still growing race, who flourish more
The more they are oppress'd; he dreads their numbers.

PRINCESS
Apis** forbid! Pharaoh afraid of Israel!
Yet should this outcast race, this helpless people
E'er grow to such a formidable greatness:
(Which all the gods avert, whom Egypt worships)
This infant's life can never serve their cause,
Nor can a single death prevent their greatness.

---

*Fane: obsolete word for temple. *(Footnotes added.)*
**Apis: A sacred bull worshipped by the ancient Egyptians.

THE COMPASSION OF PHARAOH'S DAUGHTER FOR THE INFANT MOSES
by BENJAMIN WEST, 1771

Benjamin West, American, 1738–1820. THE FINDING OF MOSES, oil on canvas, 59 x 45½ inches.
Museum purchase by exchange, Mr. William and Mr. Walter Klauer, The Snite Museum of Art, University of Notre Dame.
Used by permission.

MELITA

    I know not that: by weakest instruments
Sometimes are great events produc'd; this child
Perhaps may live to serve his upstart race
More than an host.

PRINCESS

                How ill does it beseem
Thy tender years and gentle womanhood,
To steel thy breast to pity's sacred touch!
So weak, so unprotected is our sex,
So constantly expos'd, so very helpless;
That did not Heav'n itself enjoin compassion,
Yet human policy should make us kind,
Lest we should need the pity we refuse.
Yes, I will save him——lead me to the place;
And from the feeble rushes we'll remove
The little ark, which cradles this poor babe.

*The Princess and her maid go out.*

MIRIAM *(comes forward)*

    How poor were words to speak my boundless joy!
The Princess will protect him; bless her, Heav'n!
*She looks out after the Princess, and describes her action.*

With what impatient steps she seeks the shore!
Now she approaches where the ark is laid!
With what compassion, with what angel-sweetness,
She bends to look upon the infant's face!
She takes his little hand in her's—he wakes—
She smiles upon him—hark! alas, he cries;
Weep on, sweet babe! weep on, till thou hast touch'd
Each chord of pity, waken'd every sense
Of melting sympathy, and stol'n her soul!
She takes him in her arms—O lovely Princess!
How goodness heightens beauty! now she clasps him
With fondness to her heart: she gives him now
With tender caution to her damsel's arms:
She points her to the palace, and again
This way the Princess bends her gracious steps:
The virgin train retire, and bear the child.

PRINCESS *(re-enters)*
    Did ever innocence and infant beauty
Plead with such dumb but powerful eloquence?
If I, a stranger feel these soft emotions,
What must the mother who expos'd him feel!
Go, fetch a woman of the Hebrew race,
That she may nurse the babe; and, by her garb,
Lo such a one is here!

MIRIAM
               Princess, all hail!
Forgive the bold intrusion of thy servant,
Who stands a charm'd spectator of thy goodness.

PRINCESS
    I have redeem'd an infant from the waves,
Whom I intend to nurture as mine own.

MIRIAM
    My transports will betray me! *(aside)*
Gen'rous Princess!

PRINCESS
    Know'st thou a matron of the Hebrew race,
To whom I may confide him?

MIRIAM
               Well I know
A prudent matron of the house of Levi;
Her name is Jochebed, the wife of Amram;
Gentle she is, and fam'd throughout her tribe
For soft humanity; full well I know
That she will rear him with a mother's love.
*(aside)* O truly spoke! a mother's love indeed!
To her despairing arms I mean to give
This precious trust; the nurse shall be the mother!

PRINCESS
    With speed conduct this matron to the palace,
Yes, I will raise him up in princely greatness,
And he shall be my son. His name be *Moses*,
For I have drawn him from the perilous flood.

*They go out. She kneels.*

Thou great Unseen! thou causest gentle deeds,
And smil'st on what thou causest: thus I bless thee,
That thou didst deign consult the tender make
Of yielding human hearts, when thou ordain'dst
Humanity a virtue! Didst incline
The natural bias of the soul to mercy,
Then mad'st that mercy duty! Gracious Pow'r!
Mad'st the keen rapture exquisite as right;
Beyond the joys of sense; as pleasure sweet;
As reason constant, and as instinct strong!

## THE PLACE OF DEATH IS THE PLACE OF LIFE

We know of course, that this whole event was directed by Divine Providence. Strangely the baby was "laid in the flags, by the river's brink" at the very spot where the babies were drowned. Yet the difference here to be noted as Dr. Arthur Pink points out:

"Though Moses was brought to the place of death, he was made secure *in the ark.* And this speaks to us of Christ who went down into death for us." (Pink, *Exodus,* pages 17–18)

Dr. Pink continues his explanation of God's Providential ordering of all events:

". . . It was neither by chance nor accident that Pharaoh's daughter went down to the river that day, for there are no accidents nor chance happenings in a world presided over by the living God. Whatsoever happens in time is but the outworking of His eternal decrees—'for Whom are all things and *by* Whom are all things' (Hebrews 2:10). God is behind the scenes, ordering everything for His own glory; hence our smallest actions are controlled by Him." (Pink, *Exodus,* page 18)

Thus, in a natural way, God brought together the elements of His world to converge on the brink of the Nile, not, as it happened, on the brink of death, but on the brink of a future hope. And the emotions in the heart of the young princess were not supernatural, but supremely natural. For in the place of the cruel king there was one heart at least that did not sympathize with his ruthless policies. We believe also that God put into the heart of the Princess a willingness for Miriam to call for a Hebrew mother to nurse the child—a nurse whose wages should be paid for by the royal mother.

It is at this point in Hannah More's *Sacred Drama* of *Moses in the Bulrushes* that we see the sharp contrast between the Pagan idea of child rearing and that of a Mother of Israel. Family nurture and family education were extremely important to a people to whom the One God had been revealed. The Children of Israel had their Founding Fathers and their history of great events which formed a basis for their identity. They believed in a God of History—a God who had already intervened in the lives of their own patriarchs. While this history yet waited to be recorded—by Moses himself—yet it was known and passed down from generation to generation. It formed the most important part of the education of each new child in the family—especially of a man child. For this reason a true Mother of Israel would be concerned about the early years of child nurture for it was in those years that the precious seeds of learning one's own unique identity as a *"peculiar people"* would be planted. And with the knowledge of the Individuality of Israel would come the desire implanted in the heart and mind of each son to make some contribution to the preserving and advancing of this people so signally selected and honored by the Supreme Being. Hannah More opens her next scene with Jochebed seeking to find out what has happened to her child in the ark.

## PART THREE

JOCHEBED *(enters)*
I'VE almost reach'd the place—with cautious steps
I must approach to where the ark is laid,
Lest from the royal gardens any spy me.
—Poor babe! ere this, the pressing calls of hunger
Have broke thy short repose; the chilling waves,
Perhaps, have drench'd thy little shiv'ring limbs.
What—what must he have suffer'd! —No one sees me:
But soft, does no one listen! —Ah! how hard,
How very hard for fondness to be prudent!
Now is the moment, to embrace and feed him.
*She looks out.*
Where's Miriam? she has left her little charge;
Perhaps through fear, perhaps she was detected.
How wild is thought! how terrible conjecture!
A mother's fondness frames a thousand fears,
And shapes unreal evils into being.
*She looks toward the river.*
Ah me! where is he? soul-distracting sight!
He is not there—he's lost, he's gone, he's drown'd!
Toss'd by each beating surge my infant floats;
Cold, cold and watry is thy grave my child!
O no—I see the ark— Transporting sight!
*She goes towards it.*
What do I see? Alas the ark is empty!
The casket's left, the precious gem is gone!
You spar'd him, pitying spirits of the deep!
But vain your mercy; some insatiate beast,
Cruel as Pharaoh, took the life you spar'd—
And I shall never, never see him more!

MIRIAM *(enters)*

JOCHEBED
    Come, and lament with me thy brother's loss!

20

MIRIAM

    Come, and adore with me the GOD of Jacob!

JOCHEBED

    Miriam—the child is dead!

MIRIAM

               He lives, he lives!

JOCHEBED

    Impossible: Oh! do not mock my grief!
Seest thou that empty vessel?

MIRIAM

              From that vessel
Th' Egyptian Princess took him.

JOCHEBED

              Pharaoh's daughter?
Then still he will be slain.

MIRIAM

              His life is safe;
For know, she means to rear him as her own.

JOCHEBED
*Falls on her knees in rapture.*

    To GOD the LORD, the glory be ascrib'd!
Oh magnify'd forever be thy might,
Who mercy in a heathen's heart canst plant,
And from the depth of evil bring forth good!
*She rises.*

MIRIAM

    O blest event, beyond our warmest hopes.

JOCHEBED

    What! shall my son be nurtur'd in a court,
In princely grandeur bred? taught every art,
And every wondrous science Egypt knows?
Yet ah! I tremble, Miriam; should he learn,
With Egypt's polish'd arts, her baneful faith!

O worse exchange for death! Yes, should he learn
In yon proud palace to disown *his* hand
Who thus has sav'd him: should he e'er embrace
(As sure he will, if bred in Pharaoh's court)
The gross idolatries which Egypt owns,
Her graven images, her brutish gods;
Then shall I wish he had not been preserv'd
To shame his fathers, and deny his faith.

MIRIAM

    Then, to dispel thy fears, and crown they joy,
Hear farther wonders— Know, the gen'rous Princess
To thine own care the darling child commits.

JOCHEBED

    Speak, while my joy will give me time to listen.

MIRIAM

    By her commision'd, thou behold'st me here,
To seek a matron of the Hebrew race,
To nurse him; thou, my mother, are that matron—
I said, I knew thee well; that thou would'st rear him
Ev'n with a mother's fondness; she who bare him
(I told the Princess) could not love him more.

JOCHEBED

    Fountain of mercy! whose pervading eye
Beholds the heart, and sees what passes there,
Accept my thoughts for thanks! I have no words—
How poor were human language to express
My gratitude, my wonder, and my joy!

MIRIAM

    Yes, thou shalt pour into his infant mind
The purest precepts of the purest faith.

JOCHEBED

    O! I will fill his tender soul with virtue,
And warm his bosom with devotion's flame!
Aid me, celestial Spirit! with thy grace,
And be my labors with thy influence crown'd:
Without it they were vain. Then, then, my Miriam,

When he is furnish'd, 'gainst the evil day,
With God's whole armor,* girt with sacred truth,
And as a breast-plate, wearing righteousness,
Arm'd with the spirit of God, the shield of faith,
And with the helmet of salvation crown'd,
Inur'd to watching, and dispos'd to pray'r;
Then may I send him to a dangerous court,
And safely trust him in a perilous world,
Too full of tempting snares and fond delusions!

MIRIAM

    May bounteous Heaven thy pious cares reward!

JOCHEBED

    O Amram! O my husband! when thou come'st,
Wearied at night, to rest thee from the toils
Impos'd by haughty Pharaoh; what a tale
Have I to tell thee! yes—thy darling son
Was lost, and is restor'd; was dead, and lives!

MIRIAM

    How joyful shall we spend the live-long night
In praises to JEHOVAH, who thus mocks
All human foresight, and converts the means
Of seeming ruin into great deliverance!

JOCHEBED

    Had not my child been doom'd to such strange perils,
As a fond mother trembles to recall,
He had not been preserv'd.

MIRIAM

                And mark still farther;
Had he been sav'd by any other hand,
He had been still expos'd to equal ruin.

JOCHEBED

    Then let us join to bless the hand of Heav'n,
That this poor outcast of the house of Israel,
Condemn'd to die by Pharaoh, kept in secret

---

*I Thessalonians, chap. 5. Also Ephesians, chap. 6.

By my advent'rous fondness; then expos'd
Ev'n by that very fondness which conceal'd him,
Is now to fill the wondrous round of mercy,
Preserv'd from perishing by Pharaoh's daughter,
Sav'd by the very hand which sought to crush him!

Wise and unsearchable are all thy ways,
Thou GOD of mercies! —Lead me to my child!

THE END

———

## A GODLY MOTHER'S CONCERN

The triumphant note of Jochebed and her joy in the Providential preservation of her son by the God of Mercy rejoices our heart. Yet, we note that she would have even resigned her son to the fate of the other Hebrew sons rather than expose him to the evils and the idolatries of the corrupt Egyptian court. Remember the words which Hannah More put into her mouth?

Turin Egyptian Museum, Italy. Used by permission.

What! shall my son be nurtured in a court, . . .
Yet ah! I tremble, Miriam; should he learn,
With Egypt's polished arts, her baneful faith!
O worse exchange for death! Yes, should he learn
In yon proud palace to disown His Hand
Who thus has saved him: should he e'er embrace

(As sure he will, if bred in Pharaoh's court)
The gross idolatries which Egypt owns,
Her graven images, her brutish gods;
Then shall I wish he had not been preserved
To shame his fathers, and deny his faith.

The faith of his fathers! Jochebed was concerned lest her child forget and deny the very God – the Alone One God—who had thus preserved her son.

But the God of Moses' forefathers was superintending the events of His people and Scripture records in a few words, as it so often does, what signified the spiritual education of Moses:

"*. . . And the woman took the child, and nursed it. And the child grew, and she brought him unto Pharaoh's daughter, and he became her son. And she called his name Moses: and she said, Because I drew him out of the water.*" (Exodus 2:9–10)

Thirteen words to describe the nurture of a child! A child whose life was to unfold into the most significant life recorded in the Old Testament. Thermutus, the daughter of Pharaoh, had no children of her own so when Moses came to live and be educated in the palace, he was educated as the future King of Egypt. He became in actuality the Prince of Egypt. Yet, though destined by man for a role in the government of a pagan power, God had a greater ministry for Moses in the history of the world. But the decision would be

Moses's decision. And the Apostle Paul records in the book of Hebrews *"By faith Moses, when he was come to years, refused to be called the son of Pharaoh's daughter; Choosing rather to suffer affliction with the people of God, than to enjoy the pleasures of sin for a season; Esteeming the reproach of Christ greater riches than the treasures in Egypt: for he had respect unto the recompence of the reward."* (Hebrews 11:24–26)

What a testimony to the quality of home education which Moses received and his parents bestowed upon him that he rejected his greatest worldly opportunity for the faith of his fathers!

Alfred Edersheim in his *Bible History, Old Testament* records Moses' home nurture in these words:

"But meanwhile a precious opportunity was afforded to those believing Hebrew parents to mould the mind of the adopted son of the princess of Egypt. The three first years of life, the common eastern time for nursing, are often, even in our northern climes, where development is so much slower, a period decisive for after life. It requires no stretch of the imagination to conceive what the child Moses would learn at his mother's knee, and hear among his persecuted people. When a child so preserved and so trained found himself destined to step from his Hebrew home to the court of Pharaoh—his mind full of the promises made to the fathers, and his heart heavy with the sorrows of his brethren,—it seems almost natural that thoughts of future deliverance of his people through him should gradually rise in his soul. Many of our deepest purposes have their root in earliest childhood, and the lessons then learnt, and the thoughts then conceived, have been steadily carried out to the end of our lives." (Edersheim, *O.T.*, Vol. II, page 38)

Moses' Egyptian education and training was also under God's Directing Hand, and it too would play a part in his future contributions as legislator and historian. Edersheim comments: "St. Stephen tells us that he 'was instructed in all the wisdom of the Egyptians.' (Acts 7:22) In no country was such value attached to education, nor was it begun so early as in Egypt. No sooner was a child weaned than it was sent to school,

EGYPTIAN SCHOOL

and instructed by regularly appointed scribes. As writing was not by letters, but by hieroglyphics, which might be either pictorial representations, or symbols (a sceptre for a king, etc.), or a kind of phonetic signs, and as there seem to have been hieroglyphics for single letters, for syllables, and for words, that art alone must, from its complication, have taken almost a lifetime to master it perfectly. But beyond this, education was carried to a very great length, and, in the case of those destined for the higher professions, embraced not only the various sciences, as mathematics, astronomy, chemistry, medicine, etc., but theology, philosophy, and a knowledge of the laws. There can be no doubt that, as the adopted son of the princess, Moses would receive the highest training. Scripture tells us that, in consequence, he was 'mighty in his word and deeds,' . . ." (Edersheim, *O.T.*, Vol. II, pages 38–39)

Matthew Henry summarized Moses' Egyptian education in these words:

". . . [Moses] had the advantage of the best education and improvements of the court, with the help of which, having a great genius, he became master of all the lawful learning of the Egyptians. . . . Those whom God designs for great services he finds out ways to qualify and prepare beforehand. Moses, . . . by having his education in a learned court, (for such the Egyptian then was) is the fitter to be an historian; and by having his education in the court of Egypt is the fitter to be employed, in the name of God, as an ambassador to that court." (Henry, Vol. I, page 276)

MOSES PROTECTING JETHRO'S DAUGHTERS

Some forty years were to elapse before Moses would return to the Egyptian court. During that time God was re-educating Moses. We know that Moses, after choosing to have a part "with the people of God," had endeavored to help his brethren by carnal means. He had slain one of the Egyptian taskmasters who was mistreating *"an Hebrew, one of his brethren."* For this sin God banished him to a forty-year period of loneliness and learning. The Lord had to chasten him and to quench "the self-confidence and carnal zeal manifest in his early attempt to deliver his brethren in Egypt" to a heart ready to put full trust in the Divine methods of a Divine Deliverer. Far from the rush and excitement of a worldly court, God sent Moses to the *"back-side of the desert."* As one writer has put it:

"'The backside of the desert' is where men and things, the world and self, present circumstances and their influences, are all valued at what they are really worth. There it is, and there alone, that you will find a Divinely-adjusted balance in which to weigh all with-in and all around. . . . The heart that has found itself in the presence of God at 'the backside of the desert,' has right thoughts about everything. . . . In a word, everything is set aside save the stillness and light of the Divine presence. God's voice alone is heard. His light enjoyed, His thoughts received. This is the place to which all must go to be educated for the ministry; and there all must remain if they would succeed in the ministry. (C.H.M.)" (Pink, *Exodus*, pages 22–23)

Thus during those forty years in the desert Moses learned the reflective skills of reasoning and relating which were to be so important to him in the years when he would record the Laws of God and the history of his forefathers.

Dr. Pink again pays tribute to the early life of Moses, a life which began its critical education at home with parents. These parents we now believe made every moment instructive, planting deep the roots of his identity and individuality as a descendant of Godly forefathers.

Moses ". . . stands first among the heroes of the Old Testament. All of God's early dealings with Israel were transacted through Moses. He was a prophet, priest, and king in one person, and so united all the great and important functions which later were distributed among a plurality of persons. The history of such a one is worthy of the strictest attention, and his remarkable life deserves the closest study." (Pink, *Exodus*, page 16)

Dr. I. M. Haldeman summarizes the life of Moses in these words:

"The life of Moses presents a series of striking antitheses. He was the child of a slave, and the son of a queen. He was born in a hut, and lived in a palace. He inherited poverty, and enjoyed unlimited wealth. He was the leader of armies, and the keeper of flocks. He was the mightiest of warriors, and the meekest of men. He was educated in the court, and dwelt in the desert. He had the wisdom of Egypt, and the faith of a child. He was fitted for the city, and wandered in the wilderness. He was tempted with the pleasures of sin, and endured the hardships of virtue. He was backward in speech, and talked with God. He had the rod of a shepherd, and the power of the Infinite. He was a fugitive from Pharaoh, and an ambassador from heaven. He was the giver of the Law, and the forerunner of grace. He died alone on Mount Moab, and appeared with Christ in Judea. No man assisted at his funeral, yet God buried him." (Quoted in Pink, *Exodus*, page 16)

## THE CHILDHOOD OF MOSES SPEAKS TO US

What can we learn from the childhood of Moses that is significant to American Christians today as they educate their children at home and in school? What is the relationship of the family to the future of our nation. Certainly as we study the Scriptures we can see the faith of that family and home into which God placed Moses. It was a close knit family, with a brother and sister, Aaron and Miriam, as well as a father and a mother. In this Hebrew home were learned many compelling lessons of faith in the God of their Forefathers, in His promises to Abraham, to Issac, and to Jacob. These lessons were woven into the fabric of everyday living—glimpses of which we see when Moses later exhorts his people. In his recording the life of the law and the part which it should play in family education no doubt Moses recalled his own early education and training at home. Thus his words have special significance:

*"Hear, O Israel: The Lord our God is one Lord: And thou shalt love the Lord thy God with all thine heart, and with all thy soul, and with all thy might. And these words, which I command thee this day, shall be in thine heart: And thou shalt teach them diligently unto thy children, and shalt talk of them when thou sittest in thine house, and when thou walkest by the way, and when thou liest down, and when thou risest up."* (Deuteronomy 6:4–7)

Matthew Henry enjoyed a Biblical education under his saintly father, Philip Henry. He writes these words in commentary on this passage by Moses in Deuteronomy:

"Those that love the Lord God themselves should do what they can to engage the affections of their children to him, and so to preserve the entail of religion in their families from being cut off. *Thou shalt whet them diligently upon thy children,* so some read it; frequently repeat these things to them, try all ways of instilling them into their minds, And making them pierce into their hearts; as, in whetting a knife, it is turned first on

this side, then on that. 'Be careful and exact in teaching thy children; and aim, as by whetting, to sharpen them, and put an edge on them. Teach them to thy children, not only those of thy body' (say the Jews) 'but all those that are any way under thy care and tuition.'" (Henry, Vol. I, page 751)

Josephus indicates that when Moses gave the children of Israel the laws and the constitution of government written in a book he also instructed them to teach their children these laws:

"Let the children also learn the laws, as the first thing they are taught, which will be the best thing they can be taught, and will be the cause of their future felicity." (Josephus, page 131)

Bishop Patrick observed that Moses thought his laws so very plain and easy that every father might be able to instruct his sons in it and every mother her daughters. We remember that, in their unique position of a theocracy, a nation ruled directly by God, that each member of the nation must needs be governed individually by that law. Even as a type of the New Testament dispensation, the law written on two *"tables of stone"* was to be transferred to the *"fleshy tables of the heart."* (II Corinthians 3:3)

Moses also believed that home education must include a constant remembrance of God, and he warned lest there be a forgetting:

*"Then beware lest thou forget the Lord, which brought thee forth out of the land of Egypt, from the house of bondage."* (Deuteronomy 6:12) Remembering God as the Deliverer, the Redeemer God, was a paramount home lesson to be learned—and forgotten by the Children of Israel, over and over again.

Moses knew that learning to love the Lord with heart, soul and mind, obeying His law, and not forgetting His Providential role in their history, would culminate in the righteousness of the people. Josephus called it "virtue." In other words only a righteous people, a virtuous people could carry out the admonitions of Moses. In what Josephus calls "Moses' Farewell Address," he summarizes those statements which Moses considered most important:

"....O children of Israel! there is but one source of happiness for all mankind, the favour of God; for he alone is able to give good things to those that deserve them, and to deprive those of them that sin against him; ...

"Nor do you prefer any other constitution of government before the laws now given you; neither do you disregard that way of Divine worship which you now have, nor change it for any other form: ...

"Virtue itself is indeed the principal and the first reward, and after that it bestows abundance of others; so that your exercise of virtue towards other men will make your own lives happy, and render you more glorious than foreigners can be, and procure you an undisputed reputation with posterity." (Josephus, page 129)

## MOSES AND ISRAEL'S HISTORY OF LIBERTY

The History of Liberty begins with the Providential Deliverance of Israel from its 400-years bondage to Egypt. This is the history which stands as the model of a people divinely appointed and divinely delivered. It is also the story of God's Providential Preparation of a Deliverer. Moses provides us with a Type of Jesus Christ our Saviour. In fact, as Matthew Henry states of the book of Exodus, "There are more types of Christ in this book than perhaps in any other book of the Old Testament; for Moses wrote of him, John 5:46. The way of man's reconciliation to God, and coming into covenant and communion with him by a Mediator, is here variously represented; and it is of great use to us for the illustration of the New Testament, now that we have that to assist us in the explication of the Old." (Henry, Vol. I, page 270)

The life of Moses is divided into forty-year periods:
1st forty years: were his life in Egypt.
2nd forty years: when Moses learned of God in the desert, how to be dependent upon Him. He was ready to learn God's methods.
3rd forty years: were his years of active service to the Lord as Deliverer of Israel from its bondage to Egypt, as Legislator in meeting God "face to face" and bringing to Israel the Law of God, especially the Ten Commandments which were to be a testimony for Godly government to all the world, as Historian of God's Providential dealings with Israel and as Teacher and Preacher to the Lord's people. Moses brought the Children of Israel up to the Promised Land and, according to God's will, left them in the hands of Joshua, who was designated to take them into Canaan.

Moses was taken by God *"from the plains of Moab unto the mountain of Nebo, to the top of Pisgah, that is over against Jericho. . . ."* Here God showed him the Promised Land. *"And the Lord said unto him, This is the land which I sware unto Abraham, unto Issac, and unto Jacob, saying, I will give it unto thy seed: I have caused thee to see it with thine eyes, but thou shalt not go over thither. So Moses the servant of the Lord died there in the land of Moab, according to the word of the Lord. And he buried him in a valley in the land of Moab, over against Beth-peor: but no man knoweth of his sepulchre unto this day. And Moses was an hundred and twenty years old when he died: his eye was not dim, nor his natural force abated. And the children of Israel wept for Moses in the plains of Moab for thirty days: so the days of weeping and mourning for Moses were ended."* (Deuteronomy 34:1–8)

## MOSES LEFT US A LITERARY HERITAGE

We know Moses as the first historian of Israel, the author of the *Pentateuch*—the first five books of the Bible. Moses is also the author of two Songs—in Exodus 15 and Deuteronomy 30; and in Revelation *"they sing the song of Moses the servant of God, and the song of the Lamb. . . ."* (Revelation 15:3). Moses is the author of Psalm 90.

Moses' first poetic work identified in Scripture is in Exodus 15. It is his song of praise to God for the deliverance of the Children of Israel from their enemies the Egyptians whom they have seen drowned in the Red Sea. They have walked through the Sea *"on dry ground."* In each case God has directed Moses to *"lift up thy rod, and stretch out thine hand over the sea."*

In all the world history there has never been such a remarkable chapter in the History of Liberty. America's Founding Fathers were so impressed and encouraged by this miraculous event that they wanted to incorporate it in their national symbols. A committee had been appointed to design America's Great Seal – that emblem which should identify America's Biblical convictions that God alone is the Sovereign Deliverer from tyranny. The *Journals of Congress* (Vol. V, page 690), give the proposal for one side of the Great Seal as follows, date August 20, 1776:

"On the other side of the said Great Seal should be the following Device. Pharaoh sitting in an open Chariot, a Crown on his head and a Sword in his hand passing through the divided Waters of the Red sea in pursuit of the Israelites: Rays from a Pillar of Fire in the Cloud, expressive of the divine Presence and Command, beaming on Moses who stands on the Shore, and extending his hand over the Sea causes it to overwhelm Pharaoh.

"Motto, 'Rebellion to Tyrants is Obedience to God'."

The two members of the Committee who wrote this proposal are Benjamin Franklin and Thomas Jefferson. The notes in the *Journal of Congress* (on page 691) give the wording proposed by each of these men:

"In the Jefferson Manuscripts in the Library of Congress are two notes of suggestion on this seal. One in the writing of Franklin, and the other in that of Jefferson. Franklin's note reads:

"'Moses [in the Dress of High Priest] standing on the Shore, and extending his Hand over the Sea, thereby causing the same to overwhelm Pharaoh who is sitting in an open Chariot, a Crown on his Head and a Sword in his Hand. Rays from a Pillar of Fire in the Clouds reaching to Moses, [expressing] to express that he acts by [the] Command of the Deity.

"'Motto, 'Rebellion to Tyrants is Obedience to God.'

"The note of Jefferson reads:

"'Pharaoh sitting in an open chariot, a crown on his head, and a sword in his hand passing thro' the divided waters of the Red sea in pursuit of the Israelites: rays from a pillar of fire in the cloud, expressive of the divine presence, [reach] and command, reaching to Moses who stands on the shore and, extending his hand over the sea, causes it to over whelm Pharaoh.

"Motto. 'Rebellion to tyrants is obedience to God.'"

## THE SONG OF MOSES
## THE BEGINNING

Ellicott comments:

The exodus of Israel begins and ends with the song of Moses. "With his usual modesty, Moses does not say that he composed the magnificent ode which follows; but it is scarcely conceivable that it can have had any other author. It bears a close resemblance to the Egyptian religious poetry, with which Moses—and probably no other Israelite of the time—would have been familiar from his early training; and it breathes the elevated tone of religious sentiment that was scarcely shared with Moses by any contemporary. . . . The ode is distinguished from later similar compositions by greater simplicity in the language, and greater freedom in the rhythmical arrangement. . . .

"The ode divides itself into two portions . . . ; the first retrospective, the second prospective. . . . First comes the burden, or refrain (verse 1), which was repeated at the close of each sub-division by Miriam and her choir of women (verse 21)." (O.T., Vol. I, page 241)

MOSES AND THE PARTING OF THE RED SEA
Standard Publishing Classic Bible Art Collection, #483. (Used by permission.)

## EXODUS 15, VERSES 1 TO 18
### (divisions by Ellicott, *O.T.*, Vol. I, page 241–43)

PART ONE

1 I will sing unto the LORD, for he hath triumphed gloriously: the horse and his rider hath he cast into the sea.

(Then we have the first stanza, or strophe, reaching from verse 2 to verse 5.)

*Stanza One*

2 The LORD is my strength and song, and he is become my salvation: he is my God, and I will prepare him a habitation; my fathers' God, and I will exalt him.

3 The LORD is a man of war: the LORD is his name.

4 Pharaoh's chariots and his host hath he cast into the sea: his chosen captains also are drowned in the Red sea.

5 The depths have covered them: they sank into the bottom as a stone.

(Next we have stanza or strophe 2, extending from verse 6 to verse 10.)

*Stanza Two*

6 Thy right hand, O LORD, is become glorious in power: thy right hand, O LORD, hath dashed in pieces the enemy.

7 And in the greatness of thine excellency thou has overthrown them that rose up against thee: thou sentest forth thy wrath, which consumed them as stubble.

8 And with the blast of thy nostrils the waters were gathered together, the floods stood upright as a heap, and the depths were congealed in the heart of the sea.

9 The enemy said, I will pursue, I will overtake, I will divide the spoil; my lust shall be satisfied upon them; I will draw my sword, my hand shall destroy them.

10 Thou didst blow with thy wind, the sea covered them: they sank as lead in the mighty waters.

(After this, stanza or strophe 3, comprising verses 11 and 12.)

*Stanza Three*

11 Who is like unto thee, O LORD, among the gods? who is like thee, glorious in holiness, fearful in praises, doing wonders?

12 Thou stretchedst out thy right hand, the earth swallowed them.

(These shorter, and as it were tentative, efforts are followed by the grand burst of prophetic song which constitutes Part II, and extends from verse" 13 to 18, terminating with the sublime utterance, beyond which no thought of man can go, "The Lord shall reign for ever and ever." –Ellicott, *O.T.*, Vol. I, page 241)

PART TWO

13 Thou in thy mercy hast led forth the people which thou hast redeemed: thou has guided them in thy strength unto thy holy habitation.

14 The people shall hear, and be afraid: sorrow shall take hold on the inhabitants of Palestina.

15 Then the dukes of Edom shall be amazed; the mighty men of Moab, trembling shall take hold upon them; all the inhabitants of Canaan shall melt away.

16 Fear and dread shall fall upon them; by the greatness of thine arm they shall be as still as a stone; till thy people pass over, O LORD, till the people pass over, which thou hast purchased.

17 Thou shalt bring them in, and plant them in the mountain of thine inheritance, in the place, O LORD, which thou has made for thee to dwell in; in the Sanctuary, O LORD, which thy hands have established.

18 The LORD shall reign for ever and ever.

"The concluding stanza of the ode involves a change of attitude, and deals with new matters. The poet's eye fixes itself upon the future. First, he speaks of the guidance of God, lately begun, and about to continue until Canaan is reached (verse 13). Then his glance turns to the enemies of Israel, and he considers the effect which the miraculous deliverance of Israel from Egypt will have upon them (verses 14–16). Finally, he sees the people brought into the 'land of their inheritance,' and securely established there under the ordering of Divine Providence. Then, with an ascription of glory which may be compared with the Doxology attached to the Lord's Prayer in St. Matthew, . . . he terminates his composition. (Ellicott, *O.T.*, Vol. I, page 243)

## THE SONG OF MOSES
## THE ENDING

The Book of Deuteronomy, whose name signifies "the *second law,* or a *second edition of the law,*" is the concluding book of Moses and is both a repetition and reiteration of all that Moses had delivered to Israel. What Moses spoke, Moses wrote, that "by writing, that it might abide."

As we recall, the particular reason for repeating God's pronouncements were that "the men of that generation to which the law was first given were all dead, and a new generation had sprung up, to whom God would have it repeated by Moses himself, that, if possible, it might make a lasting impression upon them." (Henry, Vol. I, page 726)

The nation Israel stood at another momentous event in their history. They were just about to take possession of the land of Canaan—the land of promise. So, while the book of Deuteronomy covers a brief period of only two months, it is a Key book in the Holy Scriptures.

Matthew Henry in his introduction summarizes:

"This book of Deuteronomy begins with a brief rehearsal of the most remarkable events that had befallen the Israelites since they came from Mount Sinai . . . . Care is taken to perpetuate the remembrance of these things among them *(ch. 31)*, particularly by a song *(ch. 32)* and so Moses concludes with a blessing *(ch. 33)*. All this was delivered by Moses to Israel in the last month of his life. The whole book contains the history of but two months . . . the latter of which was the thirty days of Israel's mourning for Moses; see how busy that great and good man was to do good when he knew that his time was short, how quick his motion when he drew near his rest. Thus we have more recorded of what our blessed Saviour said and did in the last week of his life than in any other. The last words of eminent persons make or should make deep impressions. Observe, for the honour of this book, that when our Saviour would answer the devil's temptations with, *It is written,* he fetched all his quotations out of this book, Matthew 4:4,7,10." (Henry, Vol. I, page 726)

Scripture records in the 31st chapter of Deuteronomy:

"*And the Lord said unto Moses, Behold, thou shalt sleep with thy fathers; and this people will rise up, and go a whoring after the gods of strangers of the land, whither they go to be among them, and will forsake me, and break my covenant which I have made with them. . . . Now therefore write ye this song for you, and teach it the children of Israel: put it in their mouths, that this song may be a witness for me against the children of Israel. . . . Moses therefore wrote this song the same day, and taught it the children of Israel.*" (Deuteronomy 31:16, 19, 22)

Moses' Song at the conclusion of his ministry with the children includes some of the most beautiful expressions of the nature and character of God as well as the consequences of ignoring and disobeying Him. We will illustrate a few of these passage with Matthew Henry's commentary for they represent the foundation of upon which History must build, the Rock upon which we must stand before establishing any field of study:

This song continues to verse 44 of the chapter.

A few comments from Matthew Henry:

"Now, when Moses would set forth the greatness of God, he does it, not by explaining his eternity and immensity, or describing the brightness of his glory in the upper world, but by showing the faithfulness of his word, the perfection of his works, and the wisdom and equity of all the administrations of his government; for in these his glory shines most clearly to us, and these are the things revealed concerning him, which *belong to us and our children. . . . He is the rock.* So he is called six times in this chapter, and the LXX. all along translate it . . . God. . . . God is the rock, for he is in himself immutable immovable, and he is to all that seek him and fly to him an impenetrable shelter, and to all that trust in him an everlasting foundation. . . .

"Moses, having in general represented God to them as their great benefactor, whom they were bound in gratitude to observe and obey, in these verses gives particular instances of God's kindness to them and concern for them. Some instances were ancient, and for proof of them he appeals to the records: *Remember the days of old;* that is, 'Keep in remembrance the history of those days, and of the wonderful providences of God concerning the old world, and concerning your ancestors Abraham, Isaac, and Jacob; you will find a constant series of mercies attending them, and how long since things were working towards that which was now come to pass.' Note, The authentic histories of ancient times are of singular use, and especially the history of the church in its infancy, both the Old-Testament and the New-Testament church. Others were more modern, and for proof of them he appeals to their fathers and elders that were now alive and with them. Parents must diligently teach their children, not only the word of God, his laws, and the meaning of his ordinances, but his works also, and the methods of his providence." (Henry, Vol. 1, pages 862–863)

Moses, as a last act blessed each of the particular tribes, in the tradition of Jacob. God then directed him to go ". . . up from the plains of Moab unto the mountains of Nebo, to the top of Pisgah, that is over against

MOSES ON MOUNT NEBO VIEWING THE PROMISED LAND

Jericho. . . ." God showed him the promised land saying: ". . . *This is the land which I sware unto Abraham, unto Isaac, and unto Jacob, saying, I will give it unto thy seed: I have caused thee to see it with thine eyes, but thou shalt not go over thither.*" (Deuteronomy 34:1,4)

"*And there arose not a prophet since in Israel like unto Moses, whom the Lord knew face to face. In all the signs and the wonders, which the Lord sent him to do in the land of Egypt to Pharaoh, and to all his servants, and to all his land, And in all that mighty hand, and in all the great terror which Moses showed in the sight of all Israel.*" (Deuteronomy 34:10–12)

Only once again would Moses be seen by those on earth and this is recorded by Matthew in Chapter 17: 1–3, dealing with the Transfiguration of Jesus Christ.

*"And after six days Jesus taketh Peter, James, and John his brother, and bringeth them up into a high mountain apart, And was transfigured before them: and his face did shine as the sun, and his raiment was white as the light. And, behold, there appeared unto them Moses and Elijah talking with him."*

Matthew Henry comments in part:

"It is good to be here where Christ is, and whither he brings us along with him by his appointment; it is good to be here, retired and alone with Christ; to be here, where we may behold the beauty of the Lord Jesus, Psalm 27:4. It is pleasant to hear Christ compare notes with Moses and the prophets, to see how all the institutions of the law, and all the predictions of the prophets, pointed at Christ, and were fulfilled in him." (Henry, Vol. V, page 242)

So we leave Moses as the instrument of God's deliverance of Israel, as the instrument of God's institution of law and government, and as the first historian and the author of magnificent Literature which should be our foundation for learning the relationship of the family to the nation.

# Biblical Childhood in the Old Testament

## Samuel

## &

## David

ELI INSTRUCTING SAMUEL
by Gerrit Dou (1613–1675)

# BIBLICAL CHILDHOOD IN THE OLD TESTAMENT

Of the many evidences of God's love for His people, there is no stronger continuity from Old Testament to New Testament than the Hebrew Home. Whether in captivity in a foreign land, whether in a condition of distress and decline in their own nation, the Mothers and Fathers of Israel were known throughout the centuries for a quality of home life unlike that of any other people.

We have already visualized the critical Biblical Childhood of Moses. It was in the parental home where the tender care and instruction early identified the history and character of the Children of Israel as a *"peculiar people."* It was in the home that Moses enjoyed the solicitude of a sister, Miriam, and a brother, Aaron. In Moses' home the foundations of his future mission to Israel and the world were established.

Another remarkable Biblical Childhood is that of Samuel, prophet-priest-judge of Israel, second only to Moses among the leaders raised up of God to serve the nation. Just as Moses appeared during the Egyptian captivity of Israel, so Samuel appeared at a time of spiritual decline and calamity within the nation. God always has His remnant. In each of these historic periods home made the critical contribution in forming the character of the man whom God would direct to change and challenge the external conditions of the times. In each case too, a remarkable portrait of a Mother in Israel is painted.

In Hannah, whose name "signifies grace or favour," we have another woman of faith and prayer. Her first appearance once again testifies to God's special sanction of monogamy. Hannah was only one of two wives and "the sin of polygamy" poisoned her home life, especially when it seemed that she was condemned to barrenness while her counterpart was fruitful with sons and daughters.

But Scripture indicates that Hannah's husband "loved her" in spite of her condition. He tried to ease the bitterness and frustration which "her adversary provoked." But Hannah turned away from life and in a last desperate prayer she poured out her heart to the Lord in the temple at Shiloh.

*". . . Now Eli the priest sat upon a seat by a post of the temple of the LORD. And she was in bitterness of soul, and prayed unto the LORD, and wept sore. And she vowed a vow, and said, O LORD of hosts, if thou wilt indeed look on the affliction of thine handmaid, and remember me, and not forget thine handmaid, but wilt*

*give unto thine handmaid a man child, then I will give him unto the LORD all the days of his life, and there shall no razor come upon his head."* (I Samuel 1:9–11)

As Ellicott comments on this passage:

"The vow of Hannah contained two solemn promises—the one pledged the son she prayed for to the service of the Eternal all the days of his life. The mother looked on to a life-long service in the ritual of the Tabernacle for him, but the Being who heard her prayer destined her son for higher work; in his case the priestly duties were soon merged in the far more responsible ones of the prophet—the great reformer of the people.

"The second promise undertook that he should be a Nazarite. Now the Nazariteship included three things—the refraining from intoxicating drinks, the letting the hair grow, and avoiding all ceremonial defilement . . . .

"These strange restrictions and customs had an inner signification. The abstinence from wine and strong drink typified that the Nazarite determined to avoid all sensual indulgence which might cloud the mind and render the man unfit for prayer to, and work for, the Lord; . . . the untouched hair, which here is especially mentioned, was a public protest that the consecrated one had determined to refrain from intercourse with the world, and to devote the whole strength and fulness of life to the Lord's work. . . ." (Ellicott, *O.T.*, Vol. II, page 296)

What a commentary on the condition of the nation that Eli the priest should conclude that Hannah "the weeping, praying one was a drunken woman." He, however, quickly atoned for his unworthy suspicion. The Scriptures reassure us:

*"And Hannah answered and said, No, my lord, I am a woman of a sorrowful spirit: I have drunk neither wine nor strong drink, but have poured out my soul before the LORD. Count not thine handmaid for a daughter of Belial: for out of the abundance of my complaint and grief have I spoken hitherto. Then Eli answered and said, Go in peace: and the God of Israel grant thee thy petition that thou hast asked of him. And she said,*

*Let thine handmaid find grace in thy sight. So the woman went her way, and did eat, and her countenance was no more sad."* (I Samuel 1:15–18)

In the dispensations of Divine Providence how strange and how wonderful was Eli's supporting reassurance of Hannah's heartfelt prayer and vow. How could he have known that the answer to Hannah's prayer would bring also the answer to his own helplessness as a priest of the Lord who had allowed his own sons, Hophni and Phinehas, to defile the priesthood? How could he have anticipated that God would allow him a new and pure hope for Israel in the innocence of the child who would be placed under his care and tutelage?

Hannah's child was born and named Samuel, meaning "heard of God." Scripture records that Hannah would not go up to Shiloh with her husband *". . . until the child be weaned, and then I will bring him, that he may appear before the LORD, and there abide for ever. And Elkanah her husband said unto her, Do what seemeth thee good; . . . only the LORD establish his word. So the woman abode, and gave her son suck until she weaned him."* (I Samuel 1:22–23)

One significant aspect of home nurture was the fact "that Hebrew mothers were in the habit of suckling their children for three years." Thus the child had a long and uninterrupted relationship with its mother in truest babyhood, total dependence and total reassurance between mother and child.

The fact that Hannah desired to be excused from the yearly sacrifice at the temple Matthew Henry credits to her desire ". . . not [to] be so long absent from her nursery. *Can a woman forget her suckling child?* We may suppose she kept constantly at home, for, if she had gone any where, she would have gone to Shiloh. Note, God will have mercy and not sacrifice. Those that are detained from public ordinances by the nursing and tending of little children may take comfort from this instance, and belief that, if they do that with an eye to God, he will graciously accept them therein, and though they tarry at home they shall divide the spoil." (Henry, Vol. II, page 282)

Everything is beautiful in its season. The child to be dedicated shall now ripen serenely in his own home, nestled in its mother's arms, nourished by her own milk, nurtured by her words, her warmth, and her constancy in his care and instruction.

Elkanah, the father, also plays a role in this ripening period: *"And Elkanah her husband said unto her. Do what seemeth thee good; tarry until thou have weaned him; only the LORD establish his word. . . ."* (I Samuel 1:23) Henry comments on Elkanah's prayer for the lad, saying: "that is, 'God preserve the child through the perils of his infancy, that the solemn vow which God signified his acceptance of, by giving us the child, . . . may be accomplished.'" (Henry, Vol. II, page 282)

After three years and when the child was weaned, Hannah took her son Samuel to be offered to the Lord. And with her son, Hannah also brought a sacrifice of ". . . no less than three bullocks, . . . A bullock, perhaps, for each year of the child's life. Or, one for a burnt-offering, another for a sin-offering, and the third for a peace-offering." (Henry, Vol. II, page 282)

When Hannah brought her young child to Eli, the priest, she said, joyously, to him:

*"Oh my lord, as thy soul liveth, my lord, I am the woman that stood by thee here, praying unto the LORD. For this child I prayed; and the LORD hath given me my petition which I have asked of him: Therefore also I have lent him to the LORD; as long as he liveth he shall be lent to the LORD. And he (the child) worshipped the LORD there."* (I Samuel 1:26–28) The child Samuel in worshipping the Lord there at the altar in Shiloh confirms the act ". . . thus putting his own child-seal to his mother's gift of himself to God. . . ." (Ellicott, *O.T.*, Vol II, page 298)

HANNAH PRESENTING SAMUEL TO ELI THE PRIEST

## THE SONG OF A MOTHER

Hannah joined her son at the altar of consecration even as their lives had been joined, both internally and externally, for the past years. In her prayer Hannah gave voice to one of the most beautiful Thanksgiving Songs in Scripture. Her praise to the Lord was in effect a reaffirmation of the God of Israel—whose nature and character she had taught to the young son even as he lay on her breasts as a babe. Thus early did this Mother of Israel impart to him the love and honor of the Lord and a desire to serve Him only. Certainly the words of Hannah's song form a prelude to the life and ministry of her child, Samuel.

And Hannah prayed, and said
  My heart rejoiceth in the LORD,
    mine horn is exalted in the LORD,
    my mouth is enlarged over mine enemies;
    because I rejoice in thy salvation.

There is none holy as the LORD:
    for there is none besides thee:
    neither is there any rock like our God.

Talk no more so exceedingly proudly;

let not arrogancy come out of your mouth:
for the LORD is a God of knowledge,
and by him actions are weighed.

The bows of the mighty men are broken,
and they that stumbled are girded with strength.

They that were full have hired out themselves for bread;
and they that were hungry have ceased:
so that the barren hath borne seven;
and she that hath many children is waxed feeble.

The LORD killeth, and maketh alive:
he bringeth down to the grave, and bringeth up.

The LORD maketh poor, and maketh rich:
he bringeth low, and lifteth up.

He raised up the poor out of the dust,
and lifteth up the beggar from the dunghill,
to set them among princes,
and to make them inherit the throne of glory:
for the pillars of the earth are the LORD's,
and he hath set the world upon them.

He will keep the feet of his saints,
and the wicked shall be silent in darkness;
for by his strength shall no man prevail.

The adversaries of the LORD shall be broken to pieces;
out of heaven shall be thunder upon them:
the LORD shall judge the ends of the earth;
and he shall give strength unto his king,
and exalt the horn of his anointed.

(1 Samuel 2:1–10)

## ELLICOTT'S COMMENTARY ON HANNAH'S SONG

*"And Hannah prayed, and said.*

"'Prayed,' not quite in the sense in which we generally understand prayer. Her prayer here asks for nothing; it is rather a song of thanksgiving for the past, a song which passes into expressions of sure confidence for the future. She had been an unhappy woman; her life had been, she thought, a failure; her dearest hopes had been baffled; vexed, tormented, utterly cast down, she had fled to the Rock of Israel for help, and in the eternal pity of the Divine Friend of her people she had found rest, and then joy; out of her own individual experience the Spirit of the Lord taught her to discern the general laws of the Divine economy; she had had personal experience of the gracious government of the kind, all-pitiful God; her own mercies were a pledge to her of the gracious way in which the nation itself was led by Jehovah—were a sign by which she discerned how the Eternal not only always delivered the individual sufferer who turned to Him, but would also at all times be ever ready to succour and deliver His people.

"These true, beautiful thoughts the Spirit of the Lord first planted in Hannah's heart, and then gave her lips grace and power to utter them in the sublime language of her hymn, which became one of the loved songs of the people, and as such was handed down from father to son, from generation to generation, in Israel, in the very words which first fell from the blessed mother of the child-prophet in her quiet home of 'Ramah of the Watchers.'

*"My heart rejoiceth.*

"The first verse of four lines is the introduction to the Divine song. She would give utterance to her holy joy. Had she not received the blessing at last which all mothers in Israel so longed for?

*"Mine horn is exalted.*

"She does not mean by this, 'I am proud,' but 'I am strong'—mighty now in the gift I have received from the Lord: glorious in the consciousness 'I have a God-Friend who hears me.' The image 'horn' is taken from oxen and those animals whose strength lies in their horns. It is a favourite Hebrew symbol, and one that had become familiar to them from their long experience—dating from far-back patriarchal times—as a shepherd-people.

*"Neither is there any rock.*

"This was a favourite simile among the inspired song-writers of Israel. The image, doubtless, is a memory of the long desert wandering. The steep precipices and the strange fantastic rocks of Sinai, standing up in the midst of the shifting desert sands, supplied an ever present picture of unchangeableness, of majesty, and of security. The term rock, as applied to God, is first found in the Song of Moses (Deuteronomy 32:4, 15, 18, 30, 31, 37), where the juxtaposition of rock and salvation in verse 15—*he lightly esteemed the rock of his salvation*—seems to indicate that Hannah was acquainted with

this song or national hymn of Moses. The same phrase is frequent in the Psalms. . . .

*"A God of knowledge.*

"The Hebrew words are placed thus: *A God of knowledge is the Lord.* The Talmud quaintly comments here as follows: —Rabbi Ami says: 'Knowledge is of great price, for it is placed between two Divine names: as it is written (I Samuel 2:3), 'A God of knowledge is the Lord,' and therefore mercy is to be denied to him who has no knowledge; for it is written (Isaiah 27:11), 'It is a people of no understanding, therefore He that made them will not have mercy on them. . . .'

*"And by him actions are weighed.*

" . . . The meaning is that all men's actions are weighed by God according to their essential worth, all the motives which led to them are by Him, the All-knowing, taken into account before He weighs them.

*"The bows of the mighty men are broken.*

"God reverses human conditions, bringing low the wicked, and raising up the righteous.

"Von Gerlach writes of these verses that 'Every power which will be something in itself is destroyed by the Lord: every weakness which despairs of itself is transformed into power.' 'The bows of the heroes,' that is to say, *the heroes of the bow,* the symbol of human power being poetically put first instead of the bearer of the symbol. The next line contains the antithesis: while the heroes rejoicing in their strength are shattered, the tottering, powerless ones are by Him made strong for battle.

*"They that were full.*

"Another image to illustrate the vicissitudes of human affairs is sketched, one very familiar to the dwellers among the cornfields and vineyards of Canaan.

*"The barren hath born seven.*

"Here the thought of the inspired singer reverts to herself, and the imagery is drawn from the story of her own life. Seven children are mentioned as the full number of the Divine blessing in children (see Ruth 4:15; Jeremiah 15:9). There is a curious Jewish legend which relates how for each boy child that was born to Hannah, two of Peninnah's [Elkanah's other wife] died.

*"The Lord killeth, and maketh alive.*

"Death too and life come from this same omnipotent Lord: nothing in the affairs of men is the sport of blind chance. The reign of a Divine law administered by the God to whom Hannah prayed is universal, and guides with a strict unerring justice what are commonly called the ups and downs, the changes and chances, of this mortal life. . . .

*"The pillars of the earth.*

"And the gracious All-Ruler does these things, for He is the Creator and Upholder of the universe. . . .

*"He will keep the feet.*

"This was the comforting deduction Hannah drew from the circumstances of her life: this the grave moral reflection the Spirit of the Lord bade her put down for the support and solace of all true servants of the Eternal in coming ages. Seeing that Jehovah of Israel governs the world, the righteous have nothing really to fear; it is only the wicked and rebellious who have reason to be afraid. . . .

*"By strength shall no man prevail.*

"The same thought is expressed very grandly by the prophet, 'Not by might, nor by power, but by my Spirit, saith the Lord of hosts' (Zechariah 4:6). The Holy Ghost, in one of the sublime visions of St. Paul, taught the suffering apostle the same great truth, 'My grace is sufficient for thee: for my strength is made perfect in weakness' (II Corinthians 12:9).

*"His king . . . of his anointed.*

" . . . This is the first passage in the Old Testament which speaks of 'His Anointed,' or 'His Messiah.'. . . This song was soon evidently well known in Israel. The imagery, and in several passages the very words, are reproduced in the Psalms. . . ." (Ellicott, *O.T.*, Vol. II, pages 298-300)

Hannah's departure from Shiloh, leaving her son in the service of the Lord, did not end their relationship nor their love. Despite the fact that the Lord rewarded Hannah and Elkanah with three more sons and two daughters, *"the seed of this woman for the loan which is lent to the Lord,"* they came up to Shiloh for the yearly sacrifice, bringing gifts.

*"And Elkanah went to Ramah to his house. And the child did minister unto the LORD before Eli the priest."* (I Samuel 2:11)

As his father and mother departed to the quiet town of Ramah, Samuel's former home, he began his life under ". . . the shadow of the sanctuary, *ministering* with his child powers before the altar of the Invisible, and trained, we may well assume, in all the traditions and learning of Israel by the old high priest. . . ." (Ellicott, *O.T.*, Vol. II, page 300)

"Now the sons of Eli were sons of Belial; they knew not the LORD." (I Samuel 2:12) In six verses Scriptures gives a vivid account of the worldly and idolatrous conduct of Hophni and Phinehas. In contrast, the child Samuel shone out in the darkness and degradation of the prostitution of the high office of priesthood.

*"But Samuel ministered before the LORD, being a child, girded with a linen ephod."* (I Samuel 2:18) As Ellicott notes: "The ephod was a priestly dress, which Samuel received in a very early youth, because he had, with the high priest's formal sanction, been set apart for a life-long service before the Lord. This ephod was an official garment, consisted of two pieces, which rested on the shoulders in front and behind, and were joined at the top, and fastened about the body with a girdle." (Ellicott, *O.T.*, Vol. II, page 301)

In addition Samuel was also clad in a garment of love which his mother brought on her annual visits to the temple. This "little coat" had a Hebrew name of "m'il"—no doubt, closely resembling in shape the m'il, or robe worn by the high priest, only the little m'il of Samuel was without the costly symbolical ornaments attached to the high priestly robe.

"This strange, unusual dress was, no doubt, arranged for the boy by his protector and guardian, Eli, who looked on the child as destined for some great work in connection with the life of the chosen people. Not improbably the old man, too, well aware of the character of his own sons, hoped to train up the favoured child—whose connections with himself and the sanctuary had begun in so remarkable a manner—as his successor in the chief sacred and civil office in Israel." (Ellicott, *O.T.*, Vol. II, page 301)

Thus Hannah continued to rejoice in the fruition of her prayers and hopes. Despite her growing family she was not deprived of that one annual visit and the satisfaction of watching her son grow in his ministry to the Lord. How Gracious is our Lord—rewarding the faithfulness of parents to children and of children to parents!

We need only consider one more scene in the child life of Samuel and witness the manner in which the Lord used the innocence and purity of preparation

THE DEDICATION OF SAMUEL by Frank W. Topham (Samuel wearing the ephod)
*Book of Life.* Chicago: John Rudin & Co., 1923.

which originated in his home and in the close relationship of parents and children. In all of recorded literature, there is no scene as precious as this scene in the life of a child. It awakens in our hearts a recommitment to raise our children with a character to serve Him.

Scripture records: *"And the child Samuel grew on, and was in favour both with the Lord, and also with men."* (I Samuel 2:26) It is interesting to note that "the very expressions of the biographer of Samuel were adopted by St. Luke when, in the early chapters of his Gospel, he wishes to describe in a few striking words the boyhood and youth of Him who was far greater than the child-prophet of Israel." (Ellicott, *O.T.*, Vol. II, page 302)

Eli has received a messenger from the Most High in the character of "a man of God." This messenger of doom prophesies death and disaster to Eli and his family for his unfaithfulness in not dealing with his wicked sons, honoring them above the Lord. Also, the nation Israel shall suffer the affliction of losing the ark of God, captured by their Philistine enemies. Yet, in this message, as a symbol of God's redeeming love, God announces:

*"I will raise me up a faithful priest, that shall do according to that which is in mine heart and in mine mind: and I will build him a sure house; and he shall walk before mine anointed for ever."* (I Samuel 2:35) Thus the Lord confirms Eli's own conviction that the child-priest will succeed him, that Samuel is "the one chosen to replace him in his position of judge and guide of Israel." (Ellicott, *O.T.*, Vol. II, page 304)

Chapter three of First Samuel opens with the following words: *"And the child Samuel ministered unto the Lord before Eli. And the word of the Lord was precious in those days; there was no open vision."* (I Samuel 3:1)

In short "The word of the Lord" was rare. "Between the days of Deborah, and the nameless man of God who came with the awful message to Eli, no inspired voice seems to have spoken to the chosen people." (Ellicott, *O.T.*, Vol. II, page 304)

*"And it came to pass at that time, when Eli was laid down in his place, and his eyes began to wax dim,*

*that he could not see; And ere the lamp of God went out in the temple of the LORD, where the ark of God was, and Samuel was laid down to sleep; that the LORD called Samuel."* (I Samuel 3:2–4)

Ellicott relates a Talmud commentary which indicates that "no righteous man departs this life before another equally righteous was born. . . . The sun of Eli had not set before that of Samuel rose; as it is said 'ere the lamp of God was out.'

"It was night in the sanctuary. The high priest slept in one of the adjacent chambers, and the attendant ministers in another. In the centre, on the left of the entrance, stood the seven-branched candlestick, now  mentioned for the last time; superseded in the reign of Solomon by the separate candlesticks, but revived after the Captivity by the copy of the one candlestick with seven branches, as it is still seen on the Arch of Titus. It was the only light of the Tabernacle during the night, was solemnly lighted every evening, as in the devotions of the Eastern world, both Mussulman and Christian, and extinguished just before morning, when the doors were opened.

"In the deep silence of that early morning, before the sun had risen, when the sacred light was still burning, came through the mouth of the innocent child the doom of the house of Ithamar." (Ellicott, *O.T.*, Vol. II, page 305)

"*. . . [T]he LORD called Samuel: and he answered, Here am I. And he ran unto Eli, and said, Here am I; for thou calledst me. And he said, I called not; lie down again. And he went and lay down. And the LORD called yet again, Samuel. And Samuel arose and went to Eli, and said, Here am I; for thou didst call me. And he answered, I called not, my son; lie down again. Now Samuel did not yet know the LORD, neither was the word of the LORD yet revealed unto him. And the LORD called Samuel again the third time. And he arose and went to Eli, and said, Here am I; for thou didst call me. And Eli perceived that the LORD had called the child. Therefore Eli said unto Samuel, Go, lie down: and it*

*shall be, if he call thee, that thou shalt say, Speak LORD; for thy servant heareth. So Samuel went and lay down in his place. And the LORD came, and stood, and called as at other times, Samuel, Samuel. Then Samuel answered, Speak; for thy servant heareth."* (I Samuel 3:4–10)

Ellicott: *"The Lord called Samuel."*

"It seems probable that the voice came from out of the 'visible glory,' the Shekinah, which on that solemn night of the calling of the child-prophet, no doubt rested on its chosen earthly throne—the mercy-seat of God—which formed the top of the Ark, and which was overshadowed by the outspread wings of the golden Cherubim.

*"And Eli perceived that the Lord had called the child."*

"The whole story of the eventful night is told so naturally, the supernatural wonderfully interwoven with the common life of the sanctuary, that we forget, as we read, the strangeness of the events recorded. The sleeping child is awakened by a voice uttering his name. He

THE CALLING OF SAMUEL
Standard Publishing Classic Bible Art Collection, #475. (Used by permission.)

44

naturally supposes it is his half-blind old master summoning him. The same things occurs a second and a third time. Then it flashed upon Eli the boy had had no dream. We can well fancy the old man, when Samuel again came it, asking, 'Where did the voice you thought was mine come from?' and the boy would reply, 'From your chamber, master.' And the old high priest would remember that in the same direction, only at the extremity of the sanctuary, behind the veil, was the Ark and the seat of God. Was, then, the glory of the Lord shining there? and did the voice as in old days proceed from that sacred golden throne? So, he bade his pupil go to his chamber again, and if the voice spoke to him again, to answer, not Eli, but the invisible King—'*Speak, LORD; for thy servant heareth.*'

"*And the Lord came, and stood.*"

"Then before the boy, as he lay and waited for *the voice*, came *something*, and it stood before him. The question naturally occurs to us, *What* came and stood before the boy's couch? As a rule, we find that generally, when the Lord was pleased to take some form, the form is specified. Now, as in Abraham's case at Mamre, it was a traveller; now, as in Joshua's, an armed warrior, very frequently, as to Manoah, the form was that of an angel; here nothing is specially described. Was it not simply 'the glory' on which Moses gazed when he met the Holy One on Sinai—'the glory' which seemed to rest at times in the lightless Holy of Holies on the golden mercy-seat of the Ark of the Covenant? Was not this 'visible glory'—Shikinah, as the Hebrew termed it—which filled the chamber of the child, and from out of *this* came the voice of the Eternal, and spoke to Samuel?

"See how God loves holiness in children. The child Samuel was preferred by Him, to Eli, the aged high priest and judge." (Ellicott, *O.T.*, Vol. II, page 305)

"*And the LORD said to Samuel, Behold, I will do a thing in Israel, at which both the ears of every one that heareth it shall tingle. In that day I will perform against Eli all things which I have spoken concerning his house: when I begin, I will also make an end. For I have told him that I will judge his house for ever for the iniquity*

*which he knoweth; because his sons made themselves vile, and he restrained them not. And therefore I have sworn unto the house of Eli, that the iniquity of Eli's house shall not be purged with sacrifice nor offering for ever.*" (I Samuel 3:11–14)

Ellicott continues the commentary on this passage:

"*The ears of every one that heareth it shall tingle.*"
    "The calamity which is here referred to was the capture of the Ark of the Covenant. Neither the—death of the warrior priests, Hophni and Phinehas, nor the crushing defeat of the Hebrew army, would have so powerfully affected the people, but that the sacred symbol of the presence and protection of the invisible King should be allowed to fall into the hands of the uncircumcised Philistines, the hereditary foes of the chosen race, was a calamity unparalleled in the annals.
    "It seemed to say that God had indeed forsaken them.

"*Because his sons made themselves vile.*"
    "The enormity of the sin of Eli and his house, which was to be so fearfully punished, must be measured by the extent of the mischief it worked; well-nigh all Israel were involved in it. The fatal example the priests had set at Shiloh filtrated through the entire people; the result was, that unbelief in the Eternal was becoming general throughout the land. The old pure religion was rapidly dying out of the hearts of the men, and profligacy and covetousness of Shiloh would soon have been copied only too faithfully in all the homes of Israel. This fearful state of things was known to the high priest and judge, and still the weak and indulgent father refrained from removing his sons from their high office.

"*Shall not be purged with sacrifice.*"
    "No earthly sacrifice, bloody or unbloody, should ever purge on earth the sin of the doomed high priestly house. A great theological truth is contained in these few words. In the sacrificial theory of the Mosaic Law we see there was a *limit* to the efficacy of sacrifice after

SAMUEL RELATING TO ELI THE JUDGMENTS OF GOD UPON ELI'S HOUSE
by John Singleton Copley, 1780

The Wadsworth Atheneum Museum of Art, Hartford, Connecticut
The Ella Gallup Sumner and Mary Catlin Sumner Collection Fund
Used by permission.

a certain point in sin and evil example had been reached: a scar was printed on the life which no blood of bullock or of goat could wash away; but the quiet, though sorrowful, resignation with which the old man received the intimation of the certain earthly doom seems to indicate that Eli, sure of the love of the All-Pitiful, looked on to some other means of deliverance, devised in the counsels of the Eternal Friend of Israel, by which his deathless soul, after the earthly penalty, would be reconciled to the invisible King. Did not men like Eli look on in sure and certain trust to the *one hope*? Did not these holy, though often erring, patriarchs and priests see in those far-back days, 'as in a glass darkly,' the blood of another Victim, which should cleanse the repentant and sorrowing sinner from all sin?" (Ellicott, *O.T.*, Vol. II, page 306)

How must have the child-prophet have felt as he reflected upon the truths spoken to him in the dawning light of a new day for Israel? Scripture records, and we can see in our mind's eye, the following:

*"And Samuel lay until the morning, and opened the doors of the house of the LORD. And Samuel feared to shew Eli the vision. Then Eli called Samuel, and said, Samuel, my son. And he answered, Here* am *I. And he said, What is the thing that the LORD hath said unto thee? I pray thee hide it not from me: God do so to thee, and more also, if thou hide any thing* from *me of all the things that he said unto thee. And Samuel told him every whit, and hid nothing from him. And he said, It is the LORD: let him do what seemeth him good."* (I Samuel 3:15–18)

How many of the prophets were faced with having to communicate "unwelcome truth" to those they loved and honored? But, Samuel respected his ancient mentor and faithfully revealed that which Eli had already learned. "Such a reply, and such a reception of the news of the terrible doom twice communicated to him by a direct message from the Eternal indicates that Eli, in spite of his weakness and foolish partiality for his sons, was thoroughly devoted to the Lord in his heart. He saw how deeply he had failed in his high office, how he had allowed worldly considerations to influence his conduct, how he had been tried and found wanting; and now, without a murmur, he submits to the righteous judgment of his God, he leaves himself in God's hands, and never tries to justify himself and his past conduct." (Ellicott, O.T., Vol. II, page 306)

*"And Samuel grew, and the LORD was with him, and did let none of his words fall to the ground. And all Israel from Dan even to Beersheba knew that Samuel was established to be a prophet of the LORD. And the LORD appeared again in Shiloh: for the LORD revealed himself to Samuel in Shiloh by the word of the LORD."* (I Samuel 3:19–21)

## SAMUEL'S WORK OF REVIVAL AND RESTORATION

Samuel grew up to manhood in the midst of this period of "moral degradation" in the land. He knew that first Israel must restore her home life, her national religion, and regain a consciousness of her unique individuality. There was yet one more bitter experience before the work of restoration could begin and that was the crushing defeat at Aphek and the loss of the Ark of the Covenant, earthly symbol of the throne of their unseen King.

*"'Wherefore hath the Lord smitten us?'* The people and the elders who, as we have seen above, had undertaken the war of liberty at the instigation of the young man of God, amazed at their defeat, were puzzled to understand why God was evidently not in their midst; . . ." (Ellicott, *O.T.*, Vol. II, page 307–08) But it was not the retrieval of their sacred external symbol which the people required; it was first an internal change in the hearts and homes of the nation.

It took the prophet Samuel twenty years, one generation, to re-awaken his people. First, they had to see that their defeat had come about, not through the aggressiveness of the Philistines, but through their own sinfulness and disobedience to God. Second, they had to be willing to put away their false gods and to prepare their hearts to *serve him only*. At the end of twenty years the hour of deliverance for the nation came *"and all the house of Israel lamented after the LORD."* No longer only solitary hamlets and scattered families mourned after the glorious Eternal and His pure holy worship and the life required to walk in His ways; but the heart of an entire people hungered for God's presence among them. As Samuel prayed for his people the Philistines were subdued: *". . . and they came no more into the coast of Israel: and the hand of the LORD was against the Philistines all the days of Samuel."* (1 Samuel 7:13)

Samuel's ministry to the homes of Israel convinced him that the educational level of the nation had plunged during its years of failed leadership from the priesthood. "In his long wanderings up and down among the people, during his toil in the course of his vast labour of religious restoration, he had seen how deep was the ignorance of the children of Israel. In the troublous days of the judges the arts, music, poetry, and history were unknown. The chosen race cared for none of these things.

"To remedy this state of things, Samuel founded the schools of the prophets, in order that, by their agency, the mental condition of the people, might be raised, and men trained to serve God in Church and State. . . .

"The instruction was essentially free, open to all comers, and, when educated, the prophet might return to his farm, or to some occupation connected with city life. But he was from henceforth an educated man: and he had been taught too the nature of Jehovah: how He was to be worshipped, and what was the life which every member of a covenant nation ought to lead.

"Thus Samuel's schools not only raised Israel to a higher mental level, but were the great means of maintaining the worship of Jehovah among the people. . . . But the prophetic order had in Samuel's mind another important function. It was to be a permanent public power alongside the priesthood which already existed, and of the kingly office, which he, Samuel, had inaugurated. It was intended especially to offer to the latter, when inclining to tyranny, a powerful opposition,

founded on the Divine Word. Throughout the history of Israel we find the prophetical order not merely the preachers of a high and pure morality, and a lofty, spiritual religion, but we see in them . . . the protectors of the oppressed subjects against the despotic monarch, the steady defenders of the down-trodden poor against the exacting and covetous rich.

"In one sense, they filled the position which the priesthood ought to have occupied, had the representatives of that order done their duty, but who—as Samuel well knew, not only from the past sad history of the period of the judges, but from his own personal observation at Shiloh during the life-time of Eli—had been tried, and had been found miserably wanting." (Henry, Vol. II, page 290–1)

Thus, Samuel's great work began with *revival, repentance,* and *restoration*—and it began in the families of the nation. It was a direct outcome of his own family life and preparation that sprang from the prayers of his mother, Hannah, and the faithfulness of his father, Elkanah. Samuel's first work, too, with the Schools of the Prophets allowed the nation to build back the ability to become a GOD-REMEMBERING people. It allowed for Israel to once again produce its national identity as a "peculiar people" chosen of the Lord for a special contribution to the world. Out of the Schools of the Prophets came forth:

*National poets*—extolling once more for open hearts the mercies of the Lord and his great goodness to Israel

*Annalists*—or historians, recounting the many Providential events in God's blessing to the nation

*Preachers of Patriotism*—invoking remembrance of Israel as a special nation

*Moral Teachers*—leading them back to the great rock of Mosaic morality, bursting forth into a cleansing stream of individual and national reformation

*Exponents of the Law*—dealing with the detail of obedience as set forth in the Ten Commandments

*Pastors*—comforting with the "staff and rod" these sheep of the Great Shepherd

*Politicians*—preaching the polity of God's jurisdiction and government of man and the universe, and of Israel's direct rule by God.

"But their most essential characteristic," states Ellicott of the graduates of Samuel's Schools of the Prophets was "that they were instruments of revealing God's will to man."

In summarizing the life of this boy-prophet who was appointed by God to be an instrument in His education of Israel, Ellicott concludes:

"Throughout the Book of Samuel the influence of the new order of the prophets is depicted as ever growing. Samuel, the prophet and seer, chooses the first king, and during Saul's period of loyalty to God stands by him as friend and counselor. The successor to the faithless Saul is selected and anointed again by the prophet Samuel, and the young 'anointed of the Lord,' David, receives his training and education evidently in Samuel's prophetic school. All the days of Samuel's life, the seer remained David's counselor and friend.

When Samuel had passed away, another of the order, Gad the seer, trained by Samuel, took his place by David's side; and later we see the prophet Nathan occupying the same position when David had become a mighty monarch.

" ' . . . It is the first book in Holy Scriptures which declares the incarnation of Christ as King in a particular family—the family of David. It is the first book in Scripture which announced that the kingdom founded in Him, raised up from the seed of David, would be universal and everlasting. . . .

"It was thus Samuel's lot to sketch out two of the main lines of thought which converge in Christ. The idea of the prophet and the idea of the king gain under him their shape and proportion. This is especially true as regards the latter. The king is ever in Samuel's eyes 'the Messiah,' Jehovah's Anointed One." (Henry, Vol. II, page 293)

## SAMUEL ANOINTS DAVID, THE SWEET PSALMIST OF ISRAEL

Under Samuel, God established both the schools of the prophets and the monarchy. For nearly twenty years after Israel's revival and recovery of the Ark, Samuel had judged Israel as a free nation. But, in the latter years of his life the people became dissatisfied with the corruption of Samuel's own sons and craved another form of government.

*"Then all the elders of Israel gathered themselves together, and came to Samuel unto Ramah, And said unto him, Behold, thou art old, and thy sons walk not in thy ways: now make us a king to judge us like all the nations."* (I Samuel 8:4)

"The change to an earthly sovereign had been foreseen, foretold, even arranged for, by Moses, but, in spite of all this, to one like Samuel it was very bitter. It seemed to remove the people from that solitary platform which they alone among nations had been allowed to occupy . . . it was very bitter for the hero patriot to give up for ever the splendid Hebrew ideal that his people were the subjects of the Eternal King, ruled directly by him." (Ellicott, *O.T.*, Vol. II, page 321)

But God himself comforted Samuel that the rejection was not just a rejection of Samuel, but, of far greater significance, it was a rejection of God himself. Samuel endeavored to warn Israel of "the grave changes which such an appointment as that of a sovereign over the nation would bring about in the constitution. Were they willing to exchange their Republican freedom for the condition of subjection to a sovereign who, after the manner of those other kings of foreign nation—the Pharaohs, for instance—would of course govern Israel after his own will? in other words, were they willing to give up their Republic for a Despotism?" (Ellicott, *O.T.*, Vol. II, page 322)

We know the events which took place. Samuel, under God's direction anointed Saul as King over Israel (I Samuel 10). Yet, in less than three years Saul's refusal to obey God and his overt rebellion caused Samuel to say to Saul *". . . Thou hast done foolishly: thou hast not kept the commandment of the LORD thy God, which he commanded thee: for now would the LORD have established thy kingdom upon Israel for ever. But now thy kingdom shall not continue: the LORD hath sought him a man after his own heart, and the LORD hath commanded him to be captain over his people, because thou has not kept that which the LORD commanded thee."* (I Samuel 13:13,14)

But a kingship is for life. One cannot replace a king. Only when a king dies can he be replaced. For another ten years Saul continues on his path of rebellion against God despite the entreaties of Samuel. God himself speaks to the prophet Samuel of deep disappointment in Saul:

*"Then came the word of the LORD unto Samuel, saying, It repenteth me that I have set up Saul to be king: for he is turned back from following me, and hath not performed my commandments. And it grieved Samuel; and he cried unto the LORD all night."* (I Samuel 15:10–11)

Samuel carried God's message of rejection to Saul. *"And Samuel said, Hath the LORD as great delight in burnt offerings and sacrifices, as in obeying the voice of the LORD? Behold to obey is better than sacrifice, and to hearken than the fat of rams. For rebellion is as the sin of witchcraft, and stubbornness is an iniquity and idolatry. Because thou has rejected the word of the LORD, he hath also rejected thee from being king."* (I Samuel 15:22,23)

Saul's response was to confess and repent. But, though Samuel consented to publicly worship the Lord in his company, he knew that their relationship was broken. *"And Samuel came no more to see Saul until the day of his death. . . ."* (I Samuel 15:35)

Ten more years were to go by until God instructed Samuel to anoint one of the sons of Jesse. *"And the LORD said unto Samuel, How long wilt thou mourn for Saul, seeing I have rejected him from reigning over Israel? fill thine horn with oil, and go, I will send thee to Jesse the Bethlehemite: for I have provided me a king among his sons. And Samuel said, How can I go? if Saul hear it, he will kill me. And the LORD said, Take an heifer with thee, and say, I am come to sacrifice to the LORD. And call Jesse to the sacrifice, and I will show thee what thou shalt do: and thou shalt anoint unto me him whom I name unto thee. And Samuel did*

*that which the LORD spake, and came to Bethlehem. And the elders of the town trembled at his coming, and said, Comest thou peaceably? And he said, Peaceably: I am come to sacrifice unto the LORD: sanctify yourselves, and come with me to the sacrifice. And he sanctified Jesse and his sons, and called them to sacrifice."* (I Samuel 16:1–5)

"From this day forward the village of Bethlehem obtained a strange notoriety in the annals of the world. David loved the village. . . . 'The future king never forgot the flavor of the water of the well of Bethlehem' (I Chronicles 11:17). It was Bethlehem, the cradle of the great ancestor, that was selected in the counsels of the Most High as the birthplace of Jesus Christ. . . .

"From very early times the ceremony of anointing to important offices was customary among the Hebrews. . . . Anointing, however, was the principal ceremony in the inauguration of the Hebrew kings. It belonged in so special a manner to the royal functions that the favorite designation for the king in Israel was 'the Lord's anointed.' In the case of David, the ceremony of anointing was performed three times—(1) on this occasion by Samuel, when the boy was set apart for the service of the Lord; (2) when appointed king over Judah at Hebron (II Samuel 2:4); (3) when chosen as monarch over all Israel (II Samuel 5:3). All these official personages, the priest, the prophet, and peculiarly the king, were types of the great expected Deliverer, ever known as the 'Messiah,' 'the Christ,' 'the Anointed One.'. . .

"The appearance of the aged seer, with the heifer and the long horn of holy oil, at first terrified the villagers of the quiet, secluded Bethlehem. The name and appearance of the old seer was well known in all the coasts of Israel. Why had he come thus suddenly among them? Had their still remote township then been the scene of some unknown and grave crime? What was happening in Israel, which brought Samuel the seer to little Bethlehem?

"The answer at once re-assured the villagers. He had simply come to perform the usual rite of sacrifice among them. The reasons of his coming were unknown, but his mission was one alone of blessing. There was nothing unusual in his sanctifying Jesse and his sons." (Ellicott, *O.T.*, Vol. II, pages 359–360)

*"And it came to pass, when they were come, that he looked on Eliab, and said, Surely the Lord's anointed is before him. But the Lord said unto Samuel. Look not on his countenance, or on the height of his stature; because I have refused him: for the Lord seeth not as man seeth, for man looketh on the outward appearance, but the Lord looketh on the heart."* (I Samuel 16:6–7)

Seven sons of Jesse passed before Samuel, but he received no command to anoint, and no sign was given that God had chosen one of these. Then came the famous question of Samuel's to Jesse:

SAMUEL ANOINTS DAVID, THE SON OF JESSE

*". . . Are here all thy children? And he said, There remaineth yet the youngest, and behold he keepeth the sheep. And Samuel said unto Jesse, Send and fetch him: for we will not sit down till he come hither. And he sent, and brought him in. Now he was ruddy, and withal of a beautiful countenance, and goodly to look to. And the Lord said, Arise, anoint him: for this is he. Then Samuel took the horn of oil, and anointed him in the midst of his brethren: and the Spirit of the Lord came upon David from that day forward. So Samuel rose up, and went to Ramah."* (I Samuel 16:11–13)

Ellicott comments:

"Why David was kept in the background is uncertain. He, clearly, was different to the stalwart band of elder brothers who were grouped round their father.

Although fair to look on, his beauty was of a very different type to that of his brothers, probably, compared with Saul and his own brothers, little of stature, with reddish-brown hair and a fair complexion. His father and the men of the village thought less of him than of his dark, tall brothers: at all events, Jesse thought him of too little account to present to Samuel. But, as so often, God's thoughts are not our thoughts, and in a moment Samuel saw in the ruddy shepherd boy— small of stature, and held of little account in his father's house—he beheld the future king of Israel.

"The history here simply relates the bare fact that the young shepherd was anointed in the presence of his brethren. No words of Samuel on this occasion are recorded; we are left, therefore, uncertain whether any reason was given for the choice of David, or any explanation of this peculiar anointing. It would seem most probable that Samuel kept silent for the present respecting—the high destinies of the boy standing before him, and that he merely anointed him as one chosen to be his assistant in the sacrifice he was about to offer, stating probably that the Spirit of the Lord had directed him thus to associate the young son of Jesse with himself and to adopt him in some way as a pupil in his prophetic school.

"From this time forward much of David's time was doubtless spent in Samuel's company. From him he received his training in poetry and music, for which he subsequently became distinguished; from the wise seer, too, the future king derived those early lessons of wisdom and learning which enabled him later to fill so nobly the great position for which he was thus early marked out. David was, before everything, Samuel's pupil, and the last years of that long and memorable career of the prophet were spent in moulding the life of Israel's greatest king." (Ellicott, *O.T.*, Vol. II, page 360)

Although it will be more than ten years before Saul's death and David's ascent to the throne, this moment of the anointing of David becomes also the occasion of his first meeting with King Saul. It also signals his soon appearing as the Champion of Israel in his memorable encounter with the Philistine giant, Goliath of Gath.

Scripture records:

*"But the Spirit of the LORD departed from Saul, and an evil spirit from the LORD troubled him."* (I Samuel 16:14)

Ellicott comments:

"The effect of this *descent* of the Spirit of the Lord upon David was that the shepherd boy grew up into a hero, a statesman, a scholar, and a wise, far-sighted king. The effect of the *departure* of the Spirit from Saul was that from that hour the once generous king became a prey to a gloomy melancholy, and a victim to a torturing jealousy of others, which increased as time went on, and which goaded him now and again to madness, ruining his life, and marring utterly the fair promise of his early years. . . ." (Ellicott, *O.T.*, Vol. II, page 361)

*"And Saul's servants said unto him, Behold now, an evil spirit from the God troubleth thee. Let our lord now command thy servants, which are before thee, to seek out a man, who is a cunning player on an harp: and it shall come to pass, when the evil spirit from God is upon thee, that he shall play with his hand, and thou shalt be well. And Saul said unto his servants, Provide me now a man that can play well, and bring him to me. Then answered one of the servants, and said, Behold, I have seen a son of Jesse the Bethlehemite, that is cunning in playing, and a mighty valiant man, and a man of war, and prudent in matters, and a comely person, and the LORD is with him. Wherefore Saul sent messengers unto Jesse, and said, Send me David thy son, which is with the sheep. And Jesse took an ass laden with bread, and a bottle of wine, and a kid, and sent them by David his son unto Saul. And David came to Saul, and stood before him: and he loved him greatly; and he became his armourbearer. And Saul sent to Jesse, saying, Let David, I pray thee, stand before me; for he hath found favour in my sight. And it came to pass, when the evil spirit from God was upon Saul, that David took an harp, and played with his hand: so Saul was refreshed, and was well, and the evil spirit departed from him."* (I Samuel 16:15–23)

DAVID PLAYS THE HARP BEFORE SAUL by J. James Tissot

Ellicott's commentary:

"*Cunning in playing.*—As a boy, it is certain that David possessed rare gifts of poetry, and no doubt of music. It is probable that some of his early Psalms were originally composed while watching his father's sheep among those hills and vales round the village of Bethlehem, where 'in later centuries shepherds were still watching over their flocks by night, when the angel host appeared to them to tell them of the birth of a child in Bethlehem.'

"These gifts of poetry and music were further cultivated and developed in the prophets' school of Samuel, and there the young pupil of the seer no doubt quickly acquired among his companions reputation and skill which induced the 'young man' of the court of Saul to tell his afflicted master of the shepherd son of Jesse, famous for his 'cunning in playing.'

*"And a mighty valiant man, and a man of war.*

"The description of the Bethlehemite David as a mighty valiant man can well be explained from what is related in I Samuel 17:24,25, about the young shepherd's prowess in the conflicts with the lions and the bears. A question has, however, been raised respecting the expression 'a man of war' as it would seem from the narrative of chapter 17, that the combat with the giant Philistine was David's first great military exploit. It has, however, been suggested that, in addition to the combat with those wild beasts, which we know in those days frequented the thickets of the Jordan, and were a terror to the Israelitish shepherds, David had most likely been engaged in repelling one or more of the Philistine marauding expeditions so common in those wild days. Bethlehem, we know, was a strong place or garrison of these hereditary foes of Israel. . . .

*"David took an harp, and played with his hand.*

'The music,' beautifully writes F. D. Maurice, 'was more than a mere palliative. It brought back for the time the sense of a true order, a secret, inward harmony, an assurance that it is near every man, and that he may enter into it. . . . As the boy minstrel played, the afflicted monarch was refreshed, and the dark clouds rolled away.' . . .

"Luther speaks of this power of music over the sick and weary soul as 'one of the fairest and most glorious gifts of God, to which Satan is a bitter enemy, for it removes from the heart the weight of sorrow and the fascination of evil thoughts.' Basil's words on this subject are worth quoting:—'Psalmody is the calm of the soul, the repose of the spirit, the arbiter of peace. It silences the wave, and conciliates the whirlwind of our passions. It is an engenderer of friendship, a healer of dissension, a reconciler of enemies. It repels demons, lures the ministry of angels, shields us from nightly terrors, and refreshes us in daily toil.'" (Ellicott, *O.T.*, Vol. II, pages 361–362)

## DAVID'S FIRST SPIRITUAL AND MILITARY VICTORY

Scripture informs us that David did not remain indefinitely at the court of Saul. And while "*. . . the three eldest sons of Jesse went and followed Saul to battle: . . .*" against the Philistines, "*. . . David went and returned from Saul to feed his father's sheep at Bethlehem.*" (I Samuel 17:13,15)

In the course of time Jesse sent David to his brothers with "parched corn" and "loaves" and "cheeses." David's arrival was like that of Joseph when sent by Jacob to his brothers. Eliab, his eldest brother was angry with him for coming. But, David, turned aside the jealous remark and instead asked *"Is there not a cause?"* He could not help but respond to the public insult to the God of Israel going unchallenged. We know the story, of his desire to take on Goliath. "David felt that supernatural strength had been communicated to him by the Spirit of God, which came upon him on the day of his anointing. . . ." (Ellicott, *O.T.*, Vol. II, page 366)

And Saul, when the young shepherd boy stood before him pleading his success with the wild animals

that had threatened his flock, agreed to let him accept the challenge, for David's reliance was upon "The LORD."

Saul, "determined to omit no earthly means of securing victory" endeavored to arm David with his own armour, but David "put them off him," for he had not "proved" them.

*"And He took his staff in his hand.*

"It was a true stroke of military genius in David, this determination of his to fight only with the weapons . . . with which he was familiar. . . . 'So our Divine David, the Good Shepherd of Bethlehem, when He went forth at the temptation to meet Satan—our ghostly Goliath—chose *five stones* out of the brook. He took the five books of Moses out of the flowing stream of Judaism. He took what was solid out of what was fluid. He took what was permanent out of what was transitory. He took what was moral and perpetual out of what was ceremonial and temporary. He overthrew Satan. All Christ's answers to the tempter are *moral* precepts, taken from one Book of the Law (Deuteronomy), and He prefaced His replies with the same words, *'It is written'*; and with this sling and stone of Scripture He laid our Goliath low, . . ." (Ellicott, *O.T.*, Vol. II, page 367)

The reception of David as a challenger was met by the giant Philistine with contempt. But David's cool spiritual calm replied:

*"Thou comest to me with a sword, and with a spear, and with a shield: but I come to thee in the name of the LORD of hosts, the God of the armies of Israel, whom thou has defied. This day will the LORD deliver thee into mine hand; . . ."* (I Samuel 17:45–46)

*"For the battle is the LORD's.*

Although we possess no special ode or psalm composed by David on the occasion of this mortal combat, in which, owing to his sure trust in Jehovah, he won his never-to-be-forgotten victory, yet in many of the compositions attributed to him in the Psalter we find memories of this, his first great triumph. So in Psalm 44:6,8, we read—

> 'I will not trust in my bow,
> Neither shall my sword save me.
> In God we boast all the day long
> And praise thy name for ever.'

And in Psalm 33:16–20, we read—
> 'There is no king saved by the multitude of an host,
> A mighty man is not delivered by much strength.'
>   'Our soul waiteth for the Lord,
>   He is our help and our shield.'

*"But there was no sword in the hand of David.*

"The story of the daring of the son of Jesse, dwells, and with good reason, on the extraordinary valour and skill of the young champion of Israel. Had his heart for one instant failed him—as, indeed, it well might; had he not possessed a confidence which nothing could shake in an unseen Helper—or had his skill as a marksman failed him in the slightest degree, the Philistine

DAVID CUTS OFF THE HEAD OF GOLIATH by J. James Tissot

with one blow would have laid David lifeless at his feet. . . ." (Ellicott, *O.T.*, Vol. II, page 368)

But David ". . . prevailed over the Philistine with a sling and a stone, and smote the Philistine, and slew him; . . . And when the Philistines saw their champion dead, they fled." (I Samuel 17:50,51) But "the children of Israel, on the other hand, seeing the unarmed shepherd boy with the head of the great warrior who had so long defied them in his hand, felt that the old power had come back to them, and that once more their Invisible King was with them, so they at once, with an irresistible shout, charged their dismayed foes, and the battle, as far as the Philistines were concerned, became a total rout." (Ellicott, *O.T.*, Vol. II, page 368)

We may be puzzled as to the immediate events which follow, and by Saul's question to Abner, the Captain of the host: ". . . *Abner, whose son is this youth? And Abner said, As thy son liveth, O King, I cannot tell." And when David stood before the king, and was asked: ". . . Whose son art thou, thou young man? And David answered, I am the son of thy servant Jesse the Bethlehemite.*" (I Samuel 17:55,58)

Matthew Henry comments: "Though he had been at court formerly, yet, having been for some time absent, Saul had forgotten him, being melancholy and mindless, and little thinking that his musician would have spirit enough to be his champion; . . . And now he was introduced to the court with much greater advantages than before, in which he owned God's hand performing all things for him." (Henry, Vol. II, page 378)

David's presentation to the court was also his first presentation to the son of Saul, Jonathan.

*"And it came to pass, when he had made an end of speaking unto Saul, that the soul of Jonathan was knit with the soul of David, and Jonathan loved him as his own soul. And Saul took him that day, and would let him go no more home to his father's house. Then Jonathan and David made a covenant, because he loved him as his own soul. And Jonathan stripped himself of the robe that was upon him, and gave it to David, and his garments, even to his sword, and to his bow, and to his girdle. And David went out whithersoever Saul sent him, and behaved himself wisely: and Saul set him over the men of war, and he was accepted in the sight of all the people, and also in the sight of Saul's servants."* (I Samuel 18:1–5)

Ellicott comments:

*"Jonathan loved him as his own soul.*

". . . [T]he character of the princely son of Saul is one of the most beautiful in the Old Testament story. He was the type of a true warrior of those wild, half-barbarous times—among brave men seemingly the bravest—a perfect soldier, whether fighting as a simple man-at-arms or as the general of an army—chivalrous and generous – utterly free from jealousy—a fervid believer in the God of Israel—a devoted and loyal son— a true patriot in the highest sense of the word, who sealed a devoted life by a noble death, dying as he did fighting for his king and his people. The long and steady friendship of Jonathan no doubt had a powerful and enduring influence on the after life of the greatest of the Hebrew sovereigns. The words, the unselfish, beautiful love, and, above all, the splendid example of the ill-fated son of Saul, have no doubt given their colouring to many of the noblest utterances in David's Psalms and to not a few of the most heroic deeds in David's life.

"We read of this friendship as dating from the morrow of the first striking deed of arms performed by David when he slew the giant. It is clear, however, that

it was not the personal bravery of the boy hero, or the rare skill he showed in the encounter, which so singularly attracted Prince Jonathan. These things no one would have admired and honoured more than the son of Saul, but it needed more than splendid gallantry and rare skill to attract that great love of which we read. What won Jonathan's heart was the shepherd boy's sublime faith, his perfect childlike trust in the 'Glorious Arm' of the Lord. Jonathan and David possessed one thing in common—an intense, unswerving belief in the power of Jehovah of Israel to keep and to save all who trusted in Him.

"The two were typical Israelites, both possessing in a very high degree that intense confidence in the Mighty One of Israel which was the mainspring of the people's glory and success, and which, in the seemingly interminable days of their punishment and degradation, has been the power which has kept them still together—a people distinct, reserved yet for some mighty destiny in the unknown future.

*"Made a covenant.*

"The son of the first Hebrew king recognized in David a kindred spirit. They were one in their God, in their faith, in their devotion to the Divine will. Jonathan recognised in the young shepherd, who unarmed went out alone to meet the mighty Philistine warrior, the same spirit of sublime faith in the Invisible King which had inspired him days far back to go forth alone with his armourbearer to attack and capture the Philistine stronghold, when he spoke those memorable words which enable us to understand the character of Jonathan: 'it may be that the Lord will work for us: for there is no restraint to the Lord to save by many or by few" (I Samuel 14:6).

"The great friendship, which has been the admiration of succeeding generations, began with the strong faith in the Eternal common to the two friends. Throughout its duration the link which united them was an intense desire to do the will of Him who, as true Hebrew patriots, they felt loved Israel; and when the friends parted for the last time in the wilderness of Ziph, we are told how the elder (Jonathan) strengthened the younger (David's) 'hand in God' (1 Samuel 23:16).

*"Gave it to David.*

"It has been suggested that the reason of this gift was to enable his friend David—then poorly clad—to appear at his father's court in a fitting dress; but this kind of present was usual among friends in those remote ages. Glaucus and Diomed, for instance, exchanged armour of a very different value.

'Now change we arms, and prove to either host
We guard the friendship of the line we boast . . . .
For Diomed's brass arms, of mean device,
For which nine oxen paid (a vulgar price),
He gave his own of gold, divinely wrought:
A hundred beeves the shining purchase bought.'
*Illiad*, VI, 286–295

*"And he was accepted.*

"The historian here calls especial attention to the strange power David was able to acquire over the hearts of men. It was not only over Saul and his great son that he rapidly won influence, but in the case of his colleagues at the Court and in the army, all of whom he was rapidly outstripping in the race for honour and distinction, he seems to have disarmed all jealousy. His rapid rise to high position was evidently looked upon with general favour. This is still farther enlarged upon in the next and following verses." (Ellicott, *O.T.*, Vol. II, pages 370–371)

*"And it came to pass as they came, when David was returned from the slaughter of the Philistine, that the women came out of all the cities of Israel, singing and dancing, to meet king Saul, with tabrets, with joy, and with instruments of musick. And the women answered one another as they played, and said, Saul hath slain his thousands, and David his ten thousands. And Saul was very wroth, and the saying displeased him; and he said, They have ascribed unto David ten thousands, and to me they have ascribed but thousands: and what can he have more but the Kingdom? And Saul eyed David from that day forward."* (1 Samuel 18:6–9)

*"What can he have more but the kingdom?*

"Some years had passed since he first heard from the lips of his old prophet-friend the Divine sentence of his rejection from the kingdom. In that sad period he had doubtless been on the lookout for the one destined by the Invisible King to be his successor. This dread expectation of ruin and dethronement had been a powerful factor in the causes which had led to the unhingement of Saul's mind. Was not this gifted shepherd boy—now the idol of the people— the future hope of Israel?

*"And Saul eyed David.*

"From the hour on which the king listened to the people's lilt in honour of the young hero, in Saul's distempered mind hate alternated with love. He still in his heart longed for the presence of the only human being who could charm away his ever-increasing melancholia, but he dreaded with a fierce jealousy the growing influence of the winning and gifted man whom he had taken from the sheepfolds; and now through the rest of the records of this book we shall see how the hate gradually obscured the old love. All our memories of Saul seem bound up with his life-long murderous pursuit of David." (Ellicott, *O.T.*, Vol. II, page 371)

## SAUL'S HATRED AND PURSUIT OF DAVID

*"And Saul was afraid of David, because the LORD was with him, and was departed from Saul. . . . And David behaved himself wisely in all his ways; and the LORD was with him."* (1 Samuel 18:12,14)

We may wonder why when Scripture is so clear upon both God's and Samuel's displeasure with Saul, that he is allowed to remain on the throne of Israel for nine more years. And we may wonder also why David's elevation to the throne is to be so long delayed. Divine delays usually mean, however, God's Providential preparation of His own. During the years when David was fleeing from the wrath of Saul the Lord delivered him many times. His life was spared. He was being prepared for his own long reign of forty years. He was growing in kingly character and courage. Some of his lessons were of a positive nature—his magnanimity when he twice spared the life of Saul who fell into his hands. Some of his lessons were of a negative nature when he was tempted to seek out human solutions to his problems.

During these years the king's son, Prince Jonathan continued to extend friendship, encouragement and trust in David. And David's lonely and desolate years in the wilderness made of him a reflective, meditative individual seeking to learn from his experiences, and to use his spiritual growth as a source of the enduring Psalms which he wrote throughout his lifetime.

But the day of Saul's destruction finally came—and it came by his own hand. As Ellicott commented it was "one of those very rare instances of self-destruction among the chosen people." Saul again in battle against the Philistines was experiencing defeat, *". . . and the men of Israel fled from before the Philistines, and fell down slain in mount Gilboa. And the Philistines followed hard upon Saul and upon his sons; and the Philistines slew Jonathan, and Abinadab, and Melchishua, Saul's sons. And the battle went sore against Saul, and the archers hit him; and he was sore wounded of the archers. Then said Saul unto his armourbearer, Draw thy sword, and thrust me through therewith; lest these uncircumcised come and thrust me through, and abuse me. But his armourbearer would not; for he was sore afraid. Therefore Saul took a sword and fell upon it."* (I Samuel 31:1–4)

## DAVID'S ELEGY TO SAUL AND JONATHAN

When the messenger from the battle field related the death of Saul and Jonathan to David, he *"took hold on his clothes, and rent them; and likewise all the men that were with him: And they mourned, and wept, and fasted until even, for Saul, and for Jonathan his son, and for the people of the LORD, and for the house of Israel; because they were fallen by the sword."* (II Samuel 1:11–12)

Ellicott comments:

*"They mourned.*

"On hearing the tidings of the Amalekite, David and all his people showed the usual Oriental signs of sorrow by rending their clothes, weeping, and fasting. Although David thus heard of the death of his persistent and mortal enemy, and of his own consequent accession to the throne, yet there is not the slightest reason to doubt the reality and earnestness of his mourning. The whole narrative shows that David, not only as a patriotic Israelite, lamented the death of the king, but also felt a personal attachment to Saul, notwithstanding his long and unreasonable hostility. But Saul

did not die alone; Jonathan, David's most cherished friend, fell with him. At the same time, the whole nation over which David was hereafter to reign received a crushing defeat from their foes, and large numbers of his countrymen were slain. It has been well remarked that the only deep mourning for Saul, with the exception of the men of Jabesh-gilead, came from the man whom he had hated and persecuted as long as he lived.

*"The people of the Lord.*

"Besides his personal grief, David had both a religious and a patriotic ground for sorrow. The men who had fallen were parts of that Church of God which he so earnestly loved and served, and were also members of the commonwealth of Israel, on whose behalf he ever laboured with patriotic distinction." (Ellicott, *O.T.,* Vol. II, pages 444–445)

It was at this time that David wrote "one of the finest odes in the Old Testament." It was an elegy to perpetuate the memory of those who had fallen.

*"And David lamented with this lamentation over Saul and over Jonathan his son. . . .*

## DAVID'S ODE

"The beauty of Israel is slain upon thy high places:
>how are the mighty fallen!

Tell it not in Gath, publish it not in the streets of Askelon;
>lest the daughter of the Philistines rejoice,
>lest the daughters of the uncircumcised triumph.

Ye mountains of Gilboa, let there be no dew,
>neither let there be rain upon you, nor fields of offerings:
>for there the shield of the mighty is vilely cast away,
>the shield of Saul, as though he had not been anointed with oil.

From the blood of the slain, from the fat of the mighty,
>the bow of Jonathan turned not back,
>and the sword of Saul returned not empty.

Saul and Jonathan were lovely and pleasant in their lives,
>and in their death they were not divided:
>they were swifter than eagles,
>they were stronger than lions.

Ye daughters of Israel, weep over Saul,
>who clothed you in scarlet, with other delights;
>who put on ornaments of gold upon your apparel.

How are the mighty fallen in the midst of the battle!
O Jonathan, thou wast slain in thine high places.
I am distressed for thee, my brother Jonathan:
>very pleasant hast thou been unto me:
>thy love to me was wonderful, passing the love of women.

How are the mighty fallen, and the weapons of war perished!

(II Samuel 1:19–27)

"This elegy, composed by David 'to teach the children of Israel,' bears the general title of *Kasheth*, as so many of the Psalms have kindred inscriptions. In our text it appears as extracted from that collection of sacred heroic poetry, called *Sepher hajjashar*, 'book of the just.' It consists, after a general superscription, of two unequal stanzas, each beginning with the line: 'Alas, the heroes have fallen!' The second stanza refers specially to Jonathan, and at the close of the ode the headline is repeated, with an addition, indicating Israel's great loss. The two stanzas mark, so to speak, a descent from the deepest grief for those so brave, so closely connected, and so honoured, to expression of personal feelings for Jonathan, the closing lines sounding like the last sigh over a loss too great for utterance. Peculiarly touching is the absence in this elegy of even the faintest allusion to David's painful relations to Saul in the past. All that is merely personal seems blotted out, or rather, as if it had never existed in the heart of David. In this respect we ought to regard this ode as

SAMUEL ANOINTING DAVID KING OVER ISRAEL
Standard Publishing Classic Bible Art Collection, #214. (Used by permission.)

casting most valuable light on the real meaning and character of what are sometimes called the vindictive and imprecatory Psalms. Nor should we omit to notice, what a German divine has so aptly pointed out: that, with the exception of the lament of Jabesh-gilead, the only real mourning for Saul was on the part of David, whom the king had so bitterly persecuted to the death—reminding us in this also of David's great Antitype, Who alone of all wept over that Jerusalem which was preparing to betray and crucify Him!" (Edersheim, *O.T.*, Vol. IV, pages 151–52)

At this time David is anointed king over Judah, but the men of Israel decide to make Ishbosheth, the son of Saul, king over Israel. Thus, for seven and a half more years there was conflict between David and Israel. Finally, a violent ending to the leaders of the opposition brought Israel to David voluntarily to acknowledge him as their God-anointed choice. With this third anointing David began his long reign of thirty-three years over the united kingdom of Israel and Judah.

*"Then came all the tribes of Israel to David unto*

*Hebron, and spake, saying, Behold, we are thy bone and thy flesh. Also in time past, when Saul was king over us, thou wast he that leddest out and broughtest in Israel: and the* Lord *said to thee, Thou shalt feed my people Israel, and thou shalt be a captain over Israel. So all the elders of Israel came to the king to Hebron; and king David made a league with them in Hebron before the* Lord*: and they anointed David king over Israel. David was thirty years old when he began to reign, and he reigned forty years. In Hebron he reigned over Judah seven years and six months: and in Jerusalem he reigned thirty and three years over all Israel and Judah."* (II Samuel 5:1–5)

Arthur Pink asks the question: ". . . How did the fugitive bear this sudden change of fortune? What were the thoughts of David, what the exercises of his heart, now that this great dignity, which he never sought, became his? The answer to our question is supplied by Psalm 18 which (see the superscription) he 'spoke in the day that the Lord delivered him from *all* his enemies, and from the hand of Saul,' that is, when the Lord brought to an end the opposition of Saul's house and followers. In this Psalm the Holy Spirit has recorded the breathings of David's spirit and graciously permits us to learn of the first freshness of thankfulness and praise which filled the soul of the young king upon his accession to the throne. Here we are shown the bright spiritual beginnings of the new monarchy, and are given to see how faithfully the king remembered the vows which as an exile had been mingled with his tears. . . .

"It is blessed to note that his eighteenth Psalm is entitled 'A Psalm of David, the *servant* of the Lord,' upon which C. H. Spurgeon remarked, 'David, although at this time a king, calls himself "the servant of the Lord," but makes no mention of his royalty: hence we gather that he counted it a higher honour to be the Lord's servant than to be Judah's king. Right wisely did he judge. Being possessed of poetical genius, he *served* the Lord by composing this Psalm for the use of the Lord's house.'. . ." (Pink, *David*, pages 268–269)

This is a Psalm worthy of study. We can only refer

to a few of its magnificent passages, but we rejoice that the more closely we observe the life of David, the more we can appreciate the detail of the deliverances which he mentions. This Psalm 18 is called—

*Thanksgiving for Deliverance.*

1 I will love thee, O LORD, my strength.

2 The LORD is my rock, and my fortress, and my deliverer; my God, my strength, in whom I will trust; my buckler, and the horn of my salvation, and my high tower. . . .

6 In my distress I called upon the LORD, and cried unto my God: he heard my voice out of his temple, and my cry came before him, even unto his ears. . . .

16 He sent from above, he took me, he drew me out of many waters.

17 He delivered me from my strong enemy, and from them which hated me: for they were too strong for me.

18 They prevented me in the day of my calamity: but the LORD was my stay.

19 He brought me forth also into a large place; he delivered me, because he delighted in me.

20 The LORD rewarded me according to my righteousness; according to the cleanness of my hands hath he recompensed me.

21 For I have kept the ways of the LORD, and have not wickedly departed from my God. . . .

30 As for God, his way is perfect: the word of the LORD is tried: he is a buckler to all those that trust in him.

31 For who is God save the LORD? or who is a rock save our God?

32 It is God that girdeth me with strength, and maketh my way perfect.

33 He maketh my feet like hinds' feet, and setteth me upon my high places.

34 He teacheth my hands to war, so that a bow of steel is broken by mine arms.

35 Thou hast also given me the shield of thy salvation: and thy right hand hath holden me up, and thy gentleness hath made me great.

36 Thou has enlarged my steps under me, that my feet did not slip. . . .

In a final comment upon this magnificent ode which recurs almost word for word in II Samuel 22 at the end of David's reign, Ellicott states:

"If no other literary legacy had been left by the Hebrew race, we should have from this psalm a clear conception of the character of its poetic genius. Its wealth of metaphor, its power of vivid word-painting, its accurate observation of nature, its grandeur and force of imagination, all meet us here; but above all, the fact that the bard of Israel wrote under the mighty conviction of the power and presence of Jehovah. The phenomena of the natural world appealed to his imagination as to that of poets generally, but with this addition, that they were all manifestations of a supreme glory and goodness behind them.

"In rhythm the poem is as fine as in matter." (Ellicott, *O.T.*, Vol. II, page 109)

## DAVID'S FAREWELL ADDRESS

The history of David ends with "a summary of his life and reign in their spiritual aspect." While David's life is not at an end just yet, these words are in effect his Farewell Address to Israel and another hymn of praise to his God.

Arthur Pink identifies II Samuel 23:1–7, David's last words, as being "not so much as those merely of a *man*, but rather as being a *mouthpiece* of God, thus forming a brief appendix to his Psalms."

In II Samuel 23 we see before us not "the man of war" but *"the man after God's own heart,"* the man "who had found favor in His eyes and had been loved with an everlasting love, and thus the representative of His chosen people." (Pink, *David*, Vol. I, page 286–7)

*"Now these be the last words of David. David the son of Jesse said, and the man who was raised up on high, the anointed of the God of Jacob, and the sweet psalmist of Israel, said,"* (II Samuel 23:1).

Though David was from humble parentage yet the Lord raised him up. "He was *the anointed of the God of Jacob*, and so was serviceable to the people in their civil interests, the protection of their country and the administration of justice among them. He was *the sweet psalmist of Israel*, and so was serviceable to them in their religious exercises. He penned the psalms, set the tunes, appointed both the singers and the instruments of music, but which the devotions of good people were much excited and enlarged. . . ." (Henry, Vol. II, page 565)

*"The Spirit of the LORD spake by me, and his word was in my tongue. The God of Israel said, the Rock of Israel spake to me, He that ruleth over men must be just, ruling in the fear of God."* (II Samuel 23:2–3)

"When a king was spoken to from God he was not to be complimented with the height of his dignity and the extent of his power, but to be told his duty. 'Must is for the king,' we say, Here is a *must* for the king: *He must be just, ruling in the fear of God*; and so must all inferior magistrates in their places. Let rulers remember that they rule over men—. . . They rule over men, but under God, and for him; and therefore, . . . They

must be just, both to those over whom they rule, in allowing them their rights and properties, and between those over whom they rule, using their power to right the injured against the injurious; see Deuteronomy 1:16,17. It is not enough that they do no wrong, but they must not suffer wrong to be done. They must rule in the fear of God, that is, they must themselves be possessed with a fear of God, by which they will be effectually restrained from all acts of injustice and oppression. . . . They must also endeavor to promote the fear of God (that is the practice of religion) among those over whom they rule. The magistrate is to be the keeper of both tables, and to protect both godliness and honesty. . . ." (Henry, Vol. II, page 565)

*"And he shall be as the light of the morning without clouds; as the tender grass springing out of the earth by clear shining after rain."* (II Samuel 23:4)

"As *the light of the morning*, which is most welcome after the darkness of the night (so was David's government after Saul's . . .), which is increasing, shines more and more to the perfect day, such is the growing lustre of a good government. It is likewise compared to the tender grass, which the earth produces for the service of man; it brings with it a harvest of blessings." (Henry, Vol. II, page 565–566)

"Although my house be not so with God; *yet he hath made with me an everlasting covenant, ordered in all things, and sure: for this is all my salvation, and all my desire, although he makes it not to grow.*" (II Samuel 23:5)

". . . David's family was not so with God as is described . . . the children of godly parents are often neither so holy nor so happy as might be expected. . . . *Yet he hath made me an everlasting covenant.* . . . Of the covenant of royalty (in the type) which God made with David and his seed, touching the kingdom, Psalms 132:11,12. . . . God has made a covenant of grace with us in Jesus Christ, and we are here told, . . . That it is an *everlasting* covenant, from everlasting in the contrivance and counsel of it, and to everlasting in the continuance and consequences of it. . . . That it is *ordered*,

DAVID AND HIS HARP

well ordered in all things, admirably well, to advance the glory of God and the honour of the Mediator, together with the holiness of comfort of believers. . . . That it is *all our salvation*. Nothing but this will save us, and this is sufficient: it is this only upon which our salvation depends, . . . therefore it must be *all our desire*. Let me have an interest in this covenant and the promises of it, and I have enough, I desire no more." (Henry, Vol. II, page 566)

*"But the sons of Belial shall be all of them as thorns thrust away, because they cannot be taken with hands: But the man that shall touch them must be fenced with iron and the staff of a spear; and they shall be utterly burned with fire in the same place."* (II Samuel 23:6–7)

"Here is the doom of the sons of Belial. . . . They shall be thrust away as thorns—rejected, abandoned. They are like thorns, not to be touched with hands . . ., but must be restrained by law and the sword of justice (Psalm 32:9). . . . Now this is intended, . . . As a direction to magistrates to use their power for punishing and suppressing of wickedness. Let them *thrust away the sons of Belial*; see Psalm 101:8. . . . As a caution to magistrates, and particularly to David's sons and successors, to see that they be not themselves sons of Belial (as too many of them were), for then neither the dignity of their place nor their relation to David would secure them from being thrust away by the righteous judgments of God. Though men could not deal with them, God would. . . . As a prediction of the ruin of all the implacable enemies of Christ's kingdom. There are enemies without, that openly oppose it and fight against it, and enemies within, that secretly betray it and are false to it; both are the sons of Belial, children of the wicked one, of the serpent's seed; both are as thorns, grievous and vexatious: but both shall be so thrust away as that Christ will set up his kingdom in despite of their enmity, will go *through them* (Isaiah 27:4), and will, in due time, bless his church with such peace that there will be *no pricking brier nor grieving thorn* . . . ." (Henry, Vol. II, pages 566–7)

Thus in the history and literature of the Old Testament, David the king concludes his administration on a governmental note. While he is known as the "sweet psalmist of Israel," he is a prototype of the King to come. While David was a fallible mortal, yet his struggles to be and to do good, are reminders of the role of a ruler. *"He that ruleth over men must be just, ruling in the fear of God."* (John 14:15) Justice begins with obedience to God, and it finds its fullness in the Christian idea of man and government as introduced through the love of Christ our Lord. *"If ye love me, keep my commandments. . . . This is my commandment, That ye love one another, as I have loved you. Greater love hath no man than this, that a man lay down his life for his friends."* (John 15:12–13)

The foundations of all literature are found in the Bible and the divine summary of life and living is found in our Lord Jesus Christ. Old Testament literature gives us the highest types of men and women as well as their counterpart. New Testament literature provides us with the hope of a new nature and a Mediator who is also our Advocate before the Lord and our Challenger against the Adversary, Satan, whose efforts are always governmental in the attempt to dislodge Christ from the throne within our hearts, and to deter righteous men and women from godliness.

# BIBLICAL CHILDHOOD
## IN THE
## NEW TESTAMENT

### JOHN THE BAPTIST

### &

### OUR LORD
### JESUS CHRIST

# BIBLICAL CHILDHOOD
# IN THE NEW TESTAMENT

In the time of Jesus Christ, the home-life in which He grew up among men was one of the few marks of quality left to the Jewish nation. With the absence of the words of inspired prophets for four hundred years, it is remarkable that the Lord had preserved homes like that of Zacharias and Elizabeth, and Joseph and Mary.

Jesus said of John the Baptist: *"Verily I say unto you, Among them that are born of women there hath not risen a greater than John the Baptist: . . ."* (Matthew 11:11) And John's ministry was foretold, some 700 years before, by the prophet Isaiah: *"The voice of him that crieth in the wilderness, Prepare ye the way of the LORD, make straight in the desert a highway for our God."* (Isaiah 40:3)

John's Elijah ministry, as the forerunner of Messiah, began in a miraculous way in the Temple at Jerusalem. Here the Lord appeared to the most unlikely member of the priesthood, to the venerable Zacharias as he performed his duties of burning the incense before the altar, chosen by lot for this mediatorial act. Scripture records this event:

*"And it came to pass, that while he* [Zacharias] *executed the priest's office before God in the order of his course, According to the custom of the priest's office, his lot was to burn incense when he went into the temple of* the Lord. And the whole multitude of the people were praying without at the time of the incense. And there appeared unto him an angel of the Lord standing on the right side of the altar of incense. And when Zacharias saw him, he was troubled, and fear fell upon him. But the angel said unto him, Fear not, Zacharias: for thy prayer is heard; and thy wife Elisabeth shall bear thee a son, and thou shalt call his name John. And thou shalt have joy and gladness; and many shall rejoice at his birth. For he shall be great in the sight of the Lord, and shall drink neither wine nor strong drink; and he shall be filled with the Holy Ghost, even from his mother's womb. And many of the children of Israel shall he turn to the Lord their God. And he shall go before him in the spirit and power of Elias, to turn the hearts of the fathers to the children, and the disobedient to the wisdom of the just; to make ready a people prepared for the Lord."* (Luke 1:8–17)

To Zacharias the appearance of the Angel was overwhelming. But the message that Elizabeth was to bear their son, the fruition of their years of prayer was even more astounding. Like Abraham of old there was some doubt in his mind, thus his words:

*"And Zacharias said unto the angel, Whereby shall I know this? for I am an old man, and my wife well*

*stricken in years. And the angel answering said unto him, I am Gabriel, that stands in the presence of God; and am sent to speak unto thee, and to shew thee these glad tidings. And behold, thou shalt be dumb, and not able to speak, until the day that these things shall be performed, because thou believest not my words, which shall be fulfilled in their season."* (Luke 1:18–20)

As the words of Scripture indicate, the people who waited for Zacharias and wondered why he tarried so long in the temple, soon perceived that in his speechlessness, he had "seen a vision in temple." Indeed the visible sign which Zacharias had requested of the angel was a sign to both the waiting multitude and to Elizabeth as the couple returned to their own home in the "hill country of Judea." Once again the Lord looked to instruments of His choice who were truly righteous, walking "in those commandments which were specially binding on Israel, and in those statutes that were of universal bearing on mankind. . . .

"Such a household as that of Zacharias and Elisabeth would have all that was beautiful in the religion of the time: devotion towards God; a home of affection and purity; reverence towards all that was sacred in things Divine and human; ungrudging, self-denying, loving charity to the poor; the tenderest regard for the feelings of others, so as not to raise a blush, not to wound their hearts; above all, intense faith and hope in the higher and better future of Israel. . . ." (Edersheim, *Messiah,* page 96)

For five months Elizabeth welcomed the sacred solitude of her home and her retirement from all other fellowships but that of her God and her own heart and her husband, Zacharias. At the end of that period the angel of the Lord brought "tidings of great joy" to another woman, a kinswoman in far-off Galilee:

*"And in the sixth month the angel Gabriel was sent from God unto a city of Galilee, named Nazareth, To a virgin espoused to a man whose name was Joseph, of the house of David; and the virgin's name was Mary. And the angel came unto her, and said, Hail, thou that art highly favoured, the Lord is with thee: blessed art thou among women. And when she saw him, she was troubled*

*at his saying, and cast in her mind what manner of salutation this should be. And the angel said unto her, Fear not, Mary: for thou hast found favor with God. And, behold, thou shalt conceive in thy womb, and bring forth a son, and shalt call his name JESUS. He shall be great, and shall be called the Son of the Highest: and the Lord God shall give unto him the throne of his father David: And he shall reign over the house of Jacob forever; and of his kingdom there shall be no end. Then said Mary unto the angel, How shall this be, seeing I know not a man? And the angel answered and said unto her, The Holy Ghost shall come upon thee, and the power of the Highest shall overshadow thee: therefore also that holy thing which shall be born of thee shall be called the Son of God. And, behold, thy cousin Elisabeth, she hath also conceived a son in her old age: and this is the sixth month with her, who was barren. For with God nothing shall be impossible. And Mary said, Behold the handmaid of the Lord; be it unto me according to thy word. And the angel departed from her."* (Luke 1:26–39)

Five months had passed of Elizabeth's sacred retirement when the divine messenger, the angel Gabriel, brought tidings to her kinswoman, in "far-off Galilee." This time the announcement was made "not in the solemn grandeur of the Temple" at Jerusalem, "but in the privacy of a humble home at Nazareth." (Edersheim, *Messiah,* page 106) To Mary, a virgin of the house and lineage of David, and bethrothed to Joseph of the house and lineage of David, this message was the culmination of Israel's great hope. What struck her heart was the fact that she—she of all women—should be chosen as a humble instrument of the divine plan and fulfillment of prophecy.

Like all those who have received a divine messenger—few indeed in the history of the world—Mary was troubled at the opening words of the angel, words which identified her in a most unique and prophetic way. She was *"highly favoured,"* the Lord *"was with her"* and she was *"blessed"* among women. The next words were better understood for they referred to the prophecy of Isaiah 7:14: *"Behold a virgin shall conceive, and bear a son, and shall call his name Immanuel."*

The angel reassured Mary: "*. . . Fear not, Mary: for thou hast found favour with God. And, behold, thou shalt conceive in thy womb, and bring forth a son, and shalt call his name Jesus.*" (Luke 1:30–31)

Mary's questioning of the angel was not of the same nature as that of Zacharias, she reverently wanted to know how these things shall be and how they will relate to her approaching marriage.

Matthew Henry comments:

". . . She knew that the Messiah must be born of a *virgin*; and, if she must be his mother, she desires to know how. This was not the language of her distrust, or any doubt of what the angel said, but of a desire to be further instructed. . . .

"She shall conceive by *the power of the Holy Ghost*, whose proper work and office it is to *sanctify*, and therefore to sanctify the virgin for this purpose. The Holy Ghost is called the *power of the Highest*. . . .

"She must *ask no questions* concerning the way and manner how it shall be wrought; for the Holy Ghost, as the *power of the Highest*, shall *overshadow* her, and the *cloud* covered the tabernacle when the glory of God took possession of it, to conceal it from those that would too curiously observe the motions of it, and pry into the mystery of it. The formation of every babe in the womb, and the entrance of the spirit of life into it, is a mystery in nature; none knows *the way of the spirit, nor how the bones are formed in the womb of her that is with child*, Ecclesiastes 11:5. We were *made in secret*, Psalms 139:15,16. Much more was the formation of the child Jesus a *mystery*; without controversy, *great was the mystery of godliness, God manifest in the flesh*, I Timothy 3:16. It is a *new thing created in the earth*, (Jeremiah 31:22), concerning which we must not covet to be *wise above what is written*.

"The child she shall conceive is *a holy thing*, and therefore must not be conceived by *ordinary generation*, because he must not share in the common corruption and pollution of the human nature. He is spoken of emphatically, *That Holy Thing*, such as never was; and he shall be called *the Son of God*, as the Son of the Father by eternal generation, as an indication of

which he shall now be formed by the Holy Ghost in the present conception. His human nature must be so produced, as it was fit that should be which was taken into union with the divine nature." (Henry, Vol. V, page 585)

Mary was willing to be subject to the divine authority of the messenger, and to trust the Lord to take care of all the earthly details pertaining to her forthcoming marriage to Joseph.

"*And Mary said, Behold the handmaid of the Lord; be it unto me according to thy word. . . .*" (Luke 1:38)

How gracious is our Lord to our true needs! Mary's refuge was at hand as mentioned by the angel. ". . . [T]he relief of opening her heart to a woman, in all things like-minded, who perhaps might speak blessed words to her. And to such a one the Angel himself seemed to have directed her. . . ." (Edersheim, *Messiah,* page 107)

"*And Mary arose in those days, and went into the hill country with haste, into a city of Juda; and entered into the house of Zacharias, and saluted Elisabeth. And it came to pass, that, when Elisabeth heard the salutation of Mary, the babe leaped in her womb; and Elisabeth was filled with the Holy Ghost: And she spake out with a loud voice, and said, Blessed art thou among women, and blessed is the fruit of thy womb. And whence is this to me, that the mother of my Lord should come to me? For, lo, as soon as the voice of thy salutation sounded in mine ears, the babe leaped in my womb for joy. And blessed is she that believed: for there shall be a performance of those things which were told her from the Lord.*" (Luke 1:39–45)

"It could have been no ordinary welcome that would greet the Virgin-Mother, on entering the house of her kinswoman. Elisabeth must have learnt from her husband the destiny of their son, and hence the near Advent of the Messiah. But she could not have known either *when*, or *of whom* He would be born. When, by a sign not quite strange to Jewish expectancy,* she recognised in her near kinswoman the Mother of her Lord, her salutation was that of a mother to a mother—

---

* "According to Jewish tradition, the yet unborn infants in their mother's wombs responded by an Amen to the hymn of praise at the Red Sea. . . ." (Edersheim, *Messiah,* page 107)

THE VISITATION by Louis de Boullonge the Younger, French, 1654–1733

the mother of the 'preparer' to the mother of Him for Whom he would prepare. To be more precise: the words which, filled with the Holy Ghost, she spake, were the mother's utterance, to the mother, of the homage which her unborn babe offered to his Lord; while the answering hymn of Mary was the offering of that homage unto God. It was the antiphonal morning-psalmody of the Messianic day. . . . " (Edersheim, *Messiah,* pages 107–08)

"Elizabeth's prophecy was an echo to the virgin Mary's salutation, and this song is yet a stronger echo to that prophecy, and shows her to be no less filled with the Holy Ghost than Elizabeth was. We may suppose the blessed virgin to come in, very much fatigued with her journey; yet she forgets that, and is inspired with new life, and vigour, and joy, upon the confirmation she here meets with of her faith; and since, by this sudden inspiration and transport, she finds that this was designed to be her errand hither, weary as she is, like Abraham's servant, she would neither eat nor drink till she had told her errand." (Henry, Vol. V, page 588)

## MARY'S SONG OF PRAISE

And Mary said,
    My soul doth magnify the Lord
And my spirit hath rejoiced in my God my Saviour.
For he hath regard for the low estate of his handmaiden:
    for, behold, from henceforth all generations shall call me blessed.
For he that is mighty hath done to me great things;
    and holy is his name.
And his mercy is on them that fear him
    from generation to generation.
He hath shewed strength with his arm;
    he hath scattered the proud in the imagination of their hearts.
He hath put down the mighty from their seats,
    and exalted them of low degree.
He hath filled the hungry with good things;
    and the rich he hath sent empty away.
He hath helped his servant Israel,
    in remembrance of his mercy;
As he spake to our fathers,
    to Abraham, and to his seed for ever.

Mary's song of praise, the *Magnificat* (Luke 1:46–55), is commented upon by Ellicott in these words:

*My soul doth magnify the Lord.*

"We come to the first of the great canticles recorded by St. Luke, which, since the time of Cæsarius of Arles (A.D. 540), who first introduced them into public worship, have formed part of the hymnal treasures of Western Christendom. . . . Here the song of praise is manifestly based upon that of Hannah (1 Samuel 2:1–10), both in its opening words and in much of its substance, and is so far significant of the hopes, and, if we may so speak, studies, of the maiden of Nazareth.

*In God my Saviour.*

"We may well believe that this choice of the name was determined by the meaning of the name, implying God's work of salvation, which she had been told was to be given to her Son.

*The low estate of his handmaiden.*

"Note the recurrence of the word that had been used in verse 37, as expressing the character which she was now ready to accept, whatever it might involve.

*All generations shall call me blessed.*

"The words have, of course, been partly instrumental in bringing about their own fulfillment; but what a vision of the future they must have implied then on the part of the village maiden who uttered them! Not her kinswoman only, but all generations should join in that beatitude.

*His mercy is on them that fear him.*

"The words, as read by those for whom St. Luke wrote, would seem almost to foreshadow the Gospel of the Apostle of the Gentiles. Those that 'feared God' were to be found not only among the children of Abraham, but also among 'every nation' (Acts 10:2,35), and He would show forth His mercy to all in whom that temper should be found.

*He hath shewed strength.*

"Literally, *He wrought strength*. Here the parallelism with I Samuel 2:3 becomes very close. Of whom the speaker thought of as among the 'proud,' we cannot know. They may have been the potentates of the world in which she lived, Herod and the Emperor of Rome. They may have been the men of Jerusalem, who despised Galilee; or those of the other towns and villages of Galilee, who despised Nazareth; or, though less probably, those of Nazareth itself, who despised the carpenter and his betrothed.

*The mighty.*

"The word (that from which we get our English 'dynasty') is applied to the eunuch 'of great authority' under Candace, in Acts 8:27, and is used as a divine name in 'the blessed and only Potentate' of I Timothy 6:15.

Here it is used generally of all human rulers.

*From their seats.*

"Better, *their thrones*, as the word is for the most part translated. (Compare Matthew 19:28, and in this very chapter, verse 32.)

*Of low degree.*

"The adjective is that from which the noun translated 'low estate,' in verse 48, had been formed.

*He hath filled the hungry.*

"It is interesting to note the manner in which the song of the Virgin anticipates the beatitudes of the Sermon on the Plain as reported by Luke 6:21. The words, like those of the beatitudes, have both their literal and their spiritual fulfillments. Both those who trusted in their earthly riches, and those who gloried in their fancied spiritual wealth, were sent empty away, while the 'hungry,' those who craved for a higher blessedness, were filled with the peace and righteousness which they sought.

*He hath holpen his servant Israel.*

"Up to this point the hymn has been one of personal thanksgiving. Now we find that all the soul of the maiden of Nazareth is with her people. Her joy in the 'great things' which the Lord has done for her rests on the fact that they are 'great things' for Israel also. The word which she uses for her people is that which expresses their relation to God as 'the servant' of Jehovah, who is prominent in the later chapters of Isaiah, and is in Isaiah 41:8 identified with the nation, as elsewhere with the nation's Head (Isaiah 42:1). One may see in the utterance of this hope already seen as realised, an indication of the early date of the hymn. At the time when St. Luke wrote, the rejection, not the restoration of Israel, was the dominant thought in men's minds.

*In remembrance.*

"Literally, *in order to remember*. He helped Israel, as with the purpose to prove Himself not unmindful of His promised mercy.

*As he spake to our fathers.*

"As the sentence stands in English, the words 'Abraham and his seed' seem in apposition with 'forefathers,' and to be added as explaining it. In the Greek, however, they are in a different connection, and belong to what had gone before, the construction being as follows: 'To remember His mercy (as He spake unto our forefathers) to Abraham and his seed for ever.' The mercy that had been shown to Abraham was, as it were, working even yet." (Ellicott, *N.T.*, Vol. I, pages, 248–49)

*"And Mary abode with her about three months, and returned to her own house."* (Luke 1:56)

Both mothers rejoiced in each other and what the Lord was about to bring about in their individual lives. It was a most blessed and holy time of retreat and mutual comfort.

THE BIRTH OF ST. JOHN THE BAPTIST
by Bartolome-Esteban Murillo, 1655. Spanish, 1617–1682.
Oil on canvas, 57¾ x 74⅛
The Norton-Simon Foundation, Pasadena, California. Used by Permission.

## BIRTH OF THE FORERUNNER

*"Now Elisabeth's full time came that she should be delivered; and she brought forth a son. And her neighbours and her cousins heard how the Lord had shewed great mercy upon her; and they rejoiced with her. And it came to pass, that on the eighth day they came to circumcise the child; . . ."* (Luke 1:57–59)

"Meanwhile the long-looked-for event had taken place in the home of Zacharias. No domestic solemnity so important or so joyous as that in which, by circumcision, the child had, as it were, laid upon it the yoke of the Law, with all of duty and privilege which this implied. . . ." (Edersheim, *Messiah*, page 110)

We know that the day of circumcision was the day of the admission of the child into God's covenant with his people. This was to be a day when the silence of the centuries would be broken, first through the voice of the priest, his father.

As Scripture records when that moment in the ceremony came to give the name of the father, Zacharias,

Zacharais
Detail, THE VISITATION
Louis de Boullonge,
the Younger

to the child, there was an interruption:

" . . . [A]nd they called him Zacharias, after the name of his father. And his mother answered and said, Not so; but he shall be called John. And they said unto her, There is none of thy kindred that is called by this name. And they made signs to his father, how he would have him called. And he asked for a writing table, and wrote, saying, His name is John. And they marvelled all. And his mouth was opened immediately, and his tongue loosed, and he spake, and praised God. And fear came on all that dwelt round about them: and all these sayings were noised abroad throughout all the hill country of Judæa. And all they that heard them laid them up in their hearts, saying, What manner of child shall this be! And the hand of the Lord was with him."* (Luke 1:59–66)

Zacharias, whose last words had been words of unbelief, now burst forth into a hymn of praise *". . . filled with the Holy Ghost. . . ."* (Luke 1:67; 68–79)

## ZACHARIAS'S PROPHECY

*And his father Zacharias was filled with the Holy Ghost, and prophesied, saying:*

Blessed be the Lord God of Israel;
>    for he hath visited and redeemed his people,
And hath raised up a horn of salvation for us
>    in the house of his servant David;
As he spake by the mouth of his holy prophets,
>    which have been since the world began:
That we should be saved from our enemies,
>    and from the hand of all that hate us;
To perform the mercy promised to our fathers,
>    And to remember his holy covenant;
The oath which he sware to our father Abraham,
That he would grant unto us, that we
>    being delivered out of the hand of our enemies,
>    might serve him without fear,
In holiness and righteousness before him,
>    all the days of our life.

And thou, child, shalt be called the prophet of the Highest:
>    for thou shalt go before the face of the Lord to prepare his ways;
To give knowledge of salvation unto his people
>    by the remission of their sins,
Through the tender mercy of our God;
>    whereby the dayspring from on high hath visited us,
To give light to them that sit in darkness
>    and in the shadow of death,
>    to guide our feet into the way of peace.

(Luke 1:67–79)

## ELLICOTT'S COMMENTARY ON ZACHARIAS'S PROPHECY

*Was filled with the Holy Ghost, and prophesied.*

"The latter word appears to be used in its wider sense of an inspired utterance of praise (as, *e.g.*, in I Samuel 19:20; I Corinthians 14:24–25).

"The hymn that follows appears as the report, written, probably, by Zacharias himself, of the praises that had been uttered in the first moments of his recovered gift of speech. As such, we may think of it as expressing the pent-up thoughts of the months of silence. The fire had long been kindling, and at last he spake with his tongue.

*Blessed be the Lord God of Israel.*

"The whole hymn is, like the *Magnificat*, pre-eminently Hebrew in character, almost every phrase having its counterpart in Psalm or Prophet; and, like it, has come to take a prominent place in the devotions of the Western Churches. . . .

*Visited.*

"Better, *looked upon, regarded*. The four centuries that had passed since the last of the prophets are thought of as a time during which the 'face of the Lord' had been turned away from Israel. Now He looked on it again, not to visit them (as we more commonly use the word) for their offences, but to deliver.

*Redeemed his people.*

"Better, *wrought redemption for His people....* The next verse shows that he looked for this redemption as coming not through the child that had been born to him, but through the Son, yet unborn, of Mary.

*Hath raised up an horn of salvation.*

"The symbolism of the *horn* comes from Psalm 132:17, where it is used of the representative of the House of David, and answers to the 'Anointed' of the other clause of the verse. It originated obviously in the impression made by the horns of the bull or stag, as the symbols of strength. Here, following in the steps of the Psalmist, Zacharias uses it as a description of the coming Christ, who is to be raised up in the House of David.

*His holy prophets, which have been since the world began.*

"The words were probably more than a lofty paraphrase of the more usual language 'of old time,' 'of ancient days,' and imply a reference to the great first Gospel, as it has been called, of Genesis 3:15, as well as those made to Abraham, who is the first person named as a prophet (Genesis 20:7).

*That we should be saved from our enemies.*

"Literally, *salvation from our enemies....* The 'enemies' present to the thoughts of Zacharias may have been the Roman conquerors of Judæa; the Idumæan House of Herod may have been among 'those who hate.'

*To perform the mercy.*

"The verse has been thought, and with apparent reason, to contain a reference, after the manner of the ancient prophets (compare Isaiah 8:3; Micah 1:10–15), to the name of the speaker, of his wife, and of his child. In 'performing mercy,' we find an allusion to John or Jochanan (= 'The Lord be merciful'); in 'remembering His holy covenant,' to the name Zacharias (= 'Whom Jehovah remembers'); in the 'oath' of verse 73, to that of Elizabeth or Elisheba (= 'The oath of my God'). The play upon the words would, of course, be obvious in the original Hebrew (*i.e.,* Aramaic) of the hymn, which we have only in its Greek version.

*His holy covenant.*

"The covenant is clearly that made with Abraham in Genesis 15:18. In thus going back to that as the starting-point of the New Covenant which was to be made in Christ, Zacharias anticipates the teaching of St. Paul in Galatians 3:15–19....

*Might serve him without fear.*

"The service is that of worship as well as obedience. This was the end for which deliverance from enemies was but a means....

*In holiness and righteousness.*

"... 'Holiness' has special reference to man's relations to God; 'justice' to those which connect him with his fellow men; ...

*Thou, child, shalt be called the prophet of the Highest.*

"Note the recurrence of the same divine name that had appeared in Luke 1:32,35....

*Thou shalt go before the face of the Lord....*

*To give knowledge of salvation.*

"This, ... was to be the object of the Baptist's mission. Men had lost sight of the true nature of salvation. They were wrapt in dreams of deliverance from outward enemies, and needed to be taught that it consisted in forgiveness for the sins of the past, and power to overcome sins in the future.

*The remission of their sins.*

"Historically, this was the first utterance of the words in the Gospel records, and we may well think of it as having helped to determine the form which the work of the Baptist eventually took. It is interesting to compare it with our Lord's words at the Last Supper (Matthew 26:28), and so to think of it as being the key-note of the whole work from the beginning to the end. Different in outward form as were the ministries of the Baptist and our Lord, they agreed in this.

*Through the tender mercy.*

"Literally, *on account of the bowels of mercy of our God.* After this manner the Jews spoke of what we should call 'the heart' of God. The word was a favourite one with St. Paul, as in the Greek of II Corinthians 7:15; Philippians 1:8; 2:1; Colossians 3:12. The pity that moved the heart of God is thought of, not as the instrument through which, but that on account of which, the work of the Baptist was to be accomplished.

*The dayspring from on high.*

"The English word expresses the force of the Greek very beautifully. The dawn is seen in the East rising upward, breaking through the darkness. We must re-

member, however, that the word had acquired another specially Messianic association, through its use in the LXX version as the equivalent for the 'Branch,' 'that which springs upward,' of Jeremiah 23:5; Zechariah 3:8. Here the thought of the sunrise is prominent, and it connects itself with such predictions as, 'The glory of the Lord hath risen upon thee' (Isaiah 60:1), 'The sun of righteousness shall rise' (Malachi 4:2). What had become a Messianic name is taken in its primary sense, and turned into a parable.

*Hath visited us.* Better, *hath looked upon us. To give light to them that sit in darkness.*

"The words are an echo of those of Isaiah 9:2, which we have already met with in Matthew 4:16, . . . Here they carry on the thought of the sunrise lighting up the path of those who had sat all night long in the dark ravine, and whose feet were now guided into 'the way of peace,' that word including, as it always did, with the Hebrew, every form of blessedness. . . ." (*N.T.,* Vol. I, pages 250–51)

## A CHILD IS BORN

When Mary left Elizabeth her kinswoman and came back to Nazareth, she left the quiet security of the *"hill country"* for her first spiritual trial. She must tell Joseph that she was to bear a child *"conceived in her"* by the Holy Ghost. As the Gospel of Matthew records this, we learn of Joseph's anxiety:

*"Now the birth of Jesus Christ was on this wise: When as his mother Mary was espoused to Joseph, before they came together, she was found with child of the Holy Ghost. Then Joseph her husband, being a just man, and not willing to make her a publick example, was minded to put her away privily."* (Matthew 1:18–19)

With this understanding of the Jewish law, Edersheim comments: "However conscious of what had led to her condition, it must have been as the first sharp pang of the sword which was to pierce her soul, when she told it all to her betrothed. For, however deep his trust in her whom he had chosen for wife, only a direct Divine communication could have chased all question-

ing from his heart, and given him that assurance, which was needful in the future history of the Messiah. . . ." (Edersheim, *Messiah,* page 108)

But God in His Grace did reassure Joseph so that he could act in confidence and take Mary into immediate marriage.

*"But while he thought on these things, behold, the angel of the Lord appeared unto him in a dream, saying, Joseph, thou son of David, fear not to take unto thee Mary thy wife: for that which is conceived in her is of the Holy Ghost. And she shall bring forth a son, and thou shalt call his name JESUS: for he shall save his people from their sins."* (Matthew 1:20–21)

Like the annunciation to the virgin, the angel touched back to the Scriptural prophecy which Israel had anticipated in its long history—since Adam and Eve (Genesis 3:15). The woman's "seed," prophesied by Isaiah, was the historical and spiritual confirmation which Joseph understood.

*"Now all this was done, that it might be fulfilled which was spoken of the Lord by the prophet, saying, Behold, a virgin shall be with child, and shall bring forth a son, and they shall call his name Emmanuel, which being interpreted is, God with us. Then Joseph being raised from sleep did as the angel of the Lord had bidden him, and took unto him his wife: And he knew her not till she had brought forth her firstborn son: and he called his name JESUS."* (Matthew 1:22–25)

Two great systems of law dominated the world at the time of the birth of Jesus Christ. One was the political law of Rome which unified and centralized its growing world empire. The other was the ecclesiastical law of the Rabbis whose preoccupation with disputes, discussions, and dissertations upon the finer points of agreement and disagreement with the early writings, seemed to turn them away from any immediate anticipation of Messiah.

Rome had fallen from her own high peak of moral excellence and now depended upon massive power and military strength to dominate world history and culture. Yet, while holding the world together governmentally, and while building the architectural wonders of her time, only misery and suffering followed her wars of conquest. Imperial Rome represented liberty for only a very few.

The Jews were "governed by HEROD," ". . . who, though a Jew in outward profession, was, in point of morals and practice, a contemner of all human and divine." Perhaps because he was a "tributary to Roman people," his corruption produced government of the most "oppressive kind." He was an anathema to his people; and Josephus, historian of the Jews, repudiates his administration as one of the worst curses that could have befallen his people. (See CHOC, Vol. II, pages 101–103.)

Though the coming and birth of Jesus Christ was the fulfillment of meticulous prophetic detail, yet the Jewish establishment found no place for Him in their contemporary Messianic conception. The coming of Jesus Christ found far more acceptance in the pagan world than with His own people. In fact, the gentile world was quicker to make a place for Him than were the people who alone had the key to His ancestry and mission. Four hundred years of prophetic silence had hardened the hearts of the shepherds of the flock, and the priests, in their absorption with the intricacies of external law, sealed their eyes and their ears. Yet the world longed for relief from tyranny, oppression, and man's inhumanity to man. Mankind sorely needed a Saviour to establish the Cornerstone of Liberty.

"The Roman Empire was destitute of that unity which the Gospel gives to mankind. It was a kingdom of this world; and the human race was groaning for the better peace of '*a kingdom not of this world.*'

"Thus in the very condition of the Roman Empire, and the miserable state of its mixed population, we can recognize a negative preparation for the Gospel of Christ. This tyranny and oppression called for a *Consoler*, as much as the moral sickness of the Greeks called for a Healer: a Messiah was needed by the whole Empire as much as by the Jews, though not looked for with the same conscious expectation. . . ." (T & L, page 164)

BETHLEHEM IN JUDEA

It was an edict of Roman government that brought Joseph and Mary to Bethlehem (whose name signifies 'House of Bread'), in order to fulfill the prophecy concerning His place of birth. Taxation is ever a reminder of the power of government. Yet even in that act of gathering *"every one into his own city,"* Jewish law was being fulfilled. Joseph and Mary were both of the House of David, the royal house, and thus their presence in Bethlehem confirmed their "lineage."

ST. JOSEPH AND THE CHRIST CHILD by Carlo Francesco Nuvolone
Milan 1608–1661 From the Bob Jones University Collection. Used by Permission.

Also, in accordance with His entire ministry, the Saviour of the world had only a stable as a birthplace, with lowly domesticated creatures to warm his manger with their presence. Yet it was fitting. For what earthly palace would have been fine enough to host the arrival of His Divine Majesty? Yet while earth received Him in silence, the Heavens proclaimed the glad tidings. It was sung to humble shepherds *"abiding in the field, keeping watch over their flock by night."* Their *"flock"* was a very special flock—those sheep without blemish destined for sacrifice in the Temple.

*"And, lo, the angel of the Lord came upon them, and the glory of the Lord shone round about them: and they were sore afraid. And the angel said unto them, Fear not: for, behold, I bring you good tidings of great joy, which shall be to all people. For unto you is born this day in the city of David a Saviour, which is Christ the Lord. And this shall be a sign unto you; Ye shall find the babe wrapped in swaddling clothes, lying in a manger. And suddenly there was with the angel a multitude of the heavenly host praising God, and saying,*

*Glory to God in the highest, and on earth peace, good will toward men."* (Luke 2:9–14)

The shepherds hurried into Bethlehem to see this great wonder and each detail of the angel message came to pass; and in turn, the shepherds *"made known abroad the saying which was told them concerning this child. And all that heard it wondered at those things which were told them by the shepherds."* (Luke 2:17–18)

The joyous message of the shepherds awakened hearts pure enough to remember God's Promise of a Saviour. All that looked for salvation in Israel wondered at the things that the shepherds had heard and the babe they had found in the stable. "... And yet it seemed all so sudden, so strange. That on such slender thread, as the feeble throb of an Infant-life, the salvation of the world should hang—and no special care watch over its safety, no better shelter be provided it than a 'stable,' no other cradle than a manger! And still it is ever so. . . ." (Edersheim, Messiah, page 133)

Of all those who wondered at these things, it was Mary who pondered them in her heart. Perhaps the greatest miracle of all and the kindest act of grace was that Mary so often seemed but dimly aware of the reality of the child for Whom she was the human instrumentality. Had she known in Whose Presence she found herself—the Magnitude of it all would have been overwhelming. It would have not made possible the carrying out of those acts of life so necessary to give the Child a proper upbringing and preparation for His human and Divine mission.

The babe's first visit to the temple became an act which fulfilled the conditions of the Law of circumcision on the eighth day. And this was the day when "... the Child received the Angel-given name *Jeshua* (Jesus). "... the Holy Family went up to the Temple .... The ceremony of the redemption of the firstborn son .... consisted of the formal presentation of the child to the priest, accompanied by two short 'benedictions'—the one for the law of redemption, the other for the gift of a firstborn son, after which the redemption money was paid. . . ." (Edersheim, *Messiah*, pages 135–36)

The second rite was the purification of the mother.

*"And when the days of her purification according to the law of Moses were accomplished, they brought him to Jerusalem to present him to the Lord; (As it is written in the law of the Lord, Every male that openeth the womb shall be called holy to the Lord;) And to offer a sacrifice according to that which is said in the law of the Lord, A pair of turtledoves, or two young pigeons."* (Luke 2:22–24)

Again the Providential ordering of events. For here in the temple two more witnesses bore testimony to the Divine Child.

*"And, behold, there was a man in Jerusalem, whose name was Simeon; and the same man was just and devout, waiting for the consolation of Israel: and the Holy Ghost was upon him. And it was revealed unto him by the Holy Ghost, that he should not see death, before he had seen the Lord's Christ. And he came by the Spirit into the temple: and when the parents brought in the child Jesus, to do for him after the custom of the law, Then took he him up in his arms, and blessed God, and said, Lord, now lettest thou thy servant depart in peace, according to thy word: For mine eyes have seen thy salvation, Which thou hast prepared before the face of all people; A light to lighten the Gentiles, and the glory of thy people Israel. And Joseph and his mother marvelled at those things which were spoken of him. And Simeon blessed them, and said unto Mary his mother, Behold, this child is set for the fall and rising again of many in Israel; and for a sign which shall be spoken against; (Yea, a sword shall pierce through thy own soul also,) that the thoughts of many hearts may be revealed.*

*"And there was one Anna, a prophetess, the daughter of Phanuel, of the tribe of Aser: she was of a great age, and had lived with an husband seven years from her virginity; And she was a widow of about fourscore*

SIMEON WITH THE CHILD JESUS IN HIS ARMS by Benjamin West, 1772
Eton College Chapel. Used by Permission of the Provost and Fellows of Eton College.

*and four years, which departed not from the temple, but served God with fastings and prayers night and day. And she coming in that instant gave thanks likewise unto the Lord, and spake of him to all them that looked for redemption in Jerusalem.*

*And when they had performed all things according to the law of the Lord, they returned into Galilee, to their own city of Nazareth."* (Luke 2:25–39)

## THE COMING OF THE WISE MEN TO THE SAVIOUR

Though not known to the established hierarchy, Jesus was proclaimed to be the Messiah by those closest to the Scriptural prophecies—Anna the Prophetess and Simeon, son of Hillel and father to Gamaliel, future teacher of Saul of Tarsus. And perhaps the most moving message to the world was that recorded by the shepherds in the fields watching their flocks by night —guarding those sacrificial lambs—when they first

THE NATIVITY & THE WISEMEN GUIDED BY THE STAR (below)
by Gustave Doré

Christ. The star that brought these three kings to Jerusalem has been variously defined—but there is no doubt but that there were some bright manifestations of the conjunction of several of the planets. What seemed supernaturally bright has a logical astronomical explanation. God was calling His witnesses and they came. Whether these three kings were indeed representatives of the three great races of the sons of Noah, and were named Gaspar, Melchior, and Balthasar, is not as significant as that they were drawn from afar and came to pay tribute to the young child. Their gifts were representative of Him: Gold of his Royalty; frankincense of His Divinity; myrrh of his Humanity or of His burying.

The Magi appealed to Herod for help in finding the child, He that is born King of the Jews. Herod in turn appealed to the priests and scribes demanding of them where Scripture had recorded the place of Jesus' birth. Herod was enraged when they quoted to him the words of the prophet, Micah: *"But thou, Bethlehem Ephratah, though thou be little among the thousands of Judah, yet out of thee shall come forth unto me that is to be ruler in Israel; whose goings forth have been from of old, from everlasting."* (Micah 5:2)

heard the message proclaimed by the heavenly host: *"For unto you is born this day in the city of David a Saviour, which is Christ the Lord."* (Luke 2:11) The Lamb of God had come!

. But the Gentile world was to see and acknowledge Him also—a promise of the availability of the Saviour to a dying world.

Chapter Two of Matthew's Gospel relates the coming of *"wise men from the east to Jerusalem, Saying, Where is he that is born King of the Jews? for we have seen his star in the east, and are come to worship him."* (Matthew 2:1–2)

Up until the coming of the wise men, Herod the King and the chief priests and scribes of the people were not aware of the birth of Jesus

Threatened by the prophecy of the child ruler who was to be "born" in Bethlehem, Herod ordered the slaughter of all children under two years of age. While there may have been only twenty children thus killed the tears of Mothers weeping were the first tears connected with the advent of Jesus Christ. Up to now there had been rejoicings, hymns of praise, and thanksgiving. What did this presage? (Matthew 2:18)

*"And being warned of God in a dream that they should not return to Herod, they departed into their own country another way."*

(Matthew 2:12)

"... So ends all we know of the visit of the Magi. St. Matthew, writing for Hebrews, recorded it apparently as testifying to the kingly character of Jesus. Christendom, however, has rightly seen in it a yet deeper significance, and the 'wise men' have been regarded as the first-fruits of the outlying heathen world, the earnest of the future ingathering...." (Ellicott, *N.T.*, Vol. I, page 7)

Shortly after the departure of the Magi, Joseph in a dream was instructed by the angel of the Lord, "... *saying, Arise, and take the young child and his mother, and flee into Egypt, and be thou there until I bring thee word: for Herod will seek the young child to destroy him. When he arose, he took the young child and his mother by night, and departed into Egypt: And was there until the death of Herod: that it might be fulfilled* *which was spoken by the Lord by the prophet, saying, Out of Egypt have I called my son.* [Hosea 11:1]

*"But when Herod was dead, behold, an angel of the Lord appeareth in a dream to Joseph in Egypt, Saying, Arise, and take the young child and his mother, and go into the land of Israel: for they are dead which sought the young child's life. And he arose, and took the young child and his mother, and came to the land of Israel. But when he heard that Archelaus did reign in Judæa in the room of his father Herod, he was afraid to go thither: notwithstanding, being warned of God in a dream, he turned aside into the parts of Galilee: And he came and dwelt in a city called Nazareth: that it might be fulfilled which was spoken by the prophets, He shall be called a Nazarene."* (Matthew 2:13–15; 19–23)

## THE BIBLICAL CHILDHOOD OF JESUS

*"And the child grew, and waxed strong in spirit, filled with wisdom: and the grace of God was upon him."* (Luke 2:40)

*"And he went down with them and came to Nazareth, and was subject unto them: ...."* (Luke 2:51)

We have but the briefest record from Scripture of the Childhood and youth of Jesus Christ our Lord. Yet, he spent almost all of His life in Nazareth with His family and passed His infancy, His childhood and His youth within his Hebrew home. In fact, His entire Ministry of three years, was shaped and colored by the unique and peculiar qualities of home life in Galilee. Had Jesus not been educated in such a home He never would have been prepared to minister to a world keenly longing for the blessings which flowed from the religious principles by which He lived.

While it is not possible to penetrate the silence of the Gospels regarding the earthly preparation of our Saviour, it is possible to learn some of the influences

MADONNA OF THE CHAIR
Raphael, 1483–1520, Pitti

which characterized the Childhood and Youth of Jesus. For centuries, yea, for thousands of years, the Hebrew home had been distinct from pagan homes. While the Law of God and His demands upon men for obedience, might seem extreme to pagan mentality, to the thousands raised under the Mosaic Dispensation, God was primarily a God-Loving Deity whose Wrath was but an indication of His Care and Protection of His People. Consequently, the relationship of parents to children reflected this obedience to the law and was firm, yet tender, individualistic, not just communal.

First of all, infancy in Israel was a prolonged state of nurture, beginning with from two to three years of suckling or nursing at the mother's breast. Edersheim records eight stages in this development indicating how closely the mother and child began their life together. For some of these Edersheim refers to a particular Scripture or phrase which perhaps in the original language would seem pertinent:

## PICTORIAL EXPRESSIONS OF CHILD-LIFE DEVELOPMENT

*Jeled*: the newborn babe, ISAIAH 9:6

*Jonek*: the suckling, ISAIAH 53:2 (tender plant)

*Olel*: the suckling begins to ask for food, LAM. 4:4

*Gamul*: the weaned child, ISAIAH 28:9

*Taph*: the child clinging to its mother, ESTHER 3:7

*Elem*: a child becoming firm, ISAIAH 7:14

*Naar*: youth, literally, he who shakes off, or shakes himself free

*Bachur*: the ripened one

". . . Assuredly, those who so keenly watched child-life as to give a pictorial designation to each advancing stage of its existence, must have been fondly attached to their children." (Edersheim, *Sketches*, page 104–05)

The children of Israel believed that *"Lo, children are an heritage of the LORD,"* Psalm 127:3. Therefore, they deeply loved their children and fondly watched for each stage of their unfoldment—like buds blossoming. This was the kind of a home life which our Lord knew as He lived a Child Life with His mother, Mary, and her husband, Joseph. Just as we have read of other remarkable homes in Israel, Jochebed and Amram, the home of Moses; Hannah and Elkanah, the home of little Samuel; the remarkable home of John the Baptist with Elizabeth his mother and Zacharias his father; all these were alike in the tenderness and care with which they raised the young children—like seedlings. Children were fondled and cherished and nurtured and there was rejoicing in the Lord. Home life was pictured in the Scriptures as the most desirable state of man. And children were the crown of blessing.

Blessed is every one that feareth the LORD: that walketh in his ways.
For thou shalt eat the labour of thine hands:
 happy shalt thou be, and it shall be well with thee.
Thy wife shall be as a fruitful vine by the sides of thine house:
 thy children like olive plants round about thy table.
Behold, that thus shall the man be blessed that feareth the LORD.
The LORD shall bless thee out of Zion: and thou shalt see
 the good of Jerusalem all the days of thy life.
Yea, thou shalt see thy children's children, and peace upon Israel.

(Psalm 128)

This tender regard for children is reflected in our Lord's ministry. Perhaps the most endearing portrait which we envision are the little children gathered around him.

*"And they brought young children to him, that he should touch them: and his disciples rebuked those that brought them.*

*"But when Jesus saw it, he was much displeased, and said unto them, Suffer the little children to come unto me, and forbid them not: for of such is the kingdom of God.*

*"Verily I say unto you, Whosoever shall not receive the kingdom of God as a little child, he shall not enter therein.*

*"And he took them up in his arms, put his hands upon them, and blessed them."* (Mark 10:13–16)

Yet while children were the tender focus of home life there was a deeper bond between parent and child than just the child's physical and mental development. The spiritual nature of the household was built upon the deeply religious principles and customs of worship which permeated every act, every day, every week, and every month of the year.

"... The Sabbath meal, the kindling of the Sabbath lamp, and the setting apart a portion of the dough from the bread for the household,—these are but instances, with which every 'Taph,' as he clung to his mother's skirts, must have been familiar. Even before he could follow her in such religious household duties, his eyes must have been attracted by the *Mezuzah* attached to the door-post, as the name of the Most High on the outside of the little folded parchment was reverently touched by each who came or went, and then the fingers kissed that had come in contact with the Holy Name. Indeed, the duty of the *Mezuzah* was incumbent on women also, and one can imagine it to have been in the heathen-home of Lois and Eunice in the far-off 'dispersion,' where Timothy would first learn to wonder at, then to understand, its meaning. And what lessons for the past and for the present might not be connected with it! In popular opinion it was then the symbol of the Divine guard over Israel's

BREAD MAKING IN BIBLE TIMES
"Parable of the Leaven" by N. C. Wyeth, 1931. Used by Permission.

homes, the visible emblem of this joyous hymn: 'The Lord shall preserve thy going out and coming in, from this time forth, and even for evermore.' (Psalm 121:8)..." (Edersheim, *Messiah*, page 158)

## THE NIGHT OF ISRAEL'S BIRTH

For the children of a Covenant Nation the goal of life was to live 'godly, soberly, and righteously in this present world.' And this ideal was imprinted on heart and mind by the observance of Providential Events in the history of Israel. Perhaps the most significant for the life of the young Jesus and for His family as well as for all Israelites was the celebration for the nation.

*"This month shall be unto you the beginning of months: it shall be the first month of the year to you."* (Exodus 12:2)

As Arthur Pink comments: "... Deeply significant is this. Passover-month was to *begin* Israel's year; only from this point was their national existence to be counted. The type is accurate down to the minutest detail. The new year did not begin exactly with the

Passover-night itself, for that fell between the fourteenth and fifteenth of Nisan. Now the pascal lamb was a type of the Lord Jesus, and the chronology of the civilized world is dated back to the birth of Christ. Anno Mundi (the year of the world) has given place to Anno Domini (the year of our Lord). The coming of Christ to this earth changed the calendar, and the striking thing is that the calendar is now dated not from His death, but from His birth. . . ." (Pink, *Exodus*, page 88)

In his *Bible History: Old Testament*, Alfred Edersheim records that momentous occasion in Egypt after the ninth plague had failed to soften the heart of Pharaoh and the king said to Moses: *"Get thee from me, take heed to thyself, see my face no more; for in that day thou seest my face thou shalt die."* (Exodus 10:28)

"And Moses now took up the king's challenge, and foretold how after those terrible three days' darkness 'at midnight,' Jehovah Himself would 'go out into the midst of Egypt,' and smite every firstborn of man and beast. Then would rise through the night a great lament all over the land, from the chamber of the palace, where Pharaoh's only son . . . lay a-dying, to that of the hut where the lowliest maidservant watched the ebbing tide of her child's life.

"But in Goshen all these three days was light and festive joy. For while thick darkness lay upon Egypt, the children of Israel, as directed by God, had already on the tenth of the month—four days before the great night of woe—selected their Paschal lambs, and were in waiting for their deliverance. And alike the darkness and the light were of Jehovah—the one symbolical of His judgments, the other of His favour. . . .

"Every ordinance had been given Israel about the Paschal feast, . . . and observed by them. On the tenth day of the month *Abib* (the month of ears, so called, because in it the ears of wheat first appear), or, as it was afterwards called, *Nisan*, . . . the 'Passover' sacrifice was chosen by each household.

"This was *four* days before the 'Passover' actually took place—most probably in remembrance of the prediction to Abraham, . . . that 'in the fourth generation' the children of Israel should come again to the land of Canaan. The sacrifice might be a lamb or a kid of goats, . . . but it must be 'without blemish, a male of the first year.' Each lamb or kid should be just sufficient for the sacrificial meal of a company, so that if a family were too small, it should join with another. . . . The sacrifice was offered 'between the evenings' by each head of the company, the blood caught in a basin, and some of it 'struck' 'on the two side-posts and the upper door-post of the houses' by means of 'a branch of hyssop.' The latter is not the hyssop with which we are familiar, but most probably the *caper*, which grows abundantly in Egypt, in the desert of Sinai, and in Palestine. In ancient times this plant was regarded as possessing cleansing properties. The direction, to sprinkle the entrance, meant that the blood was to be applied to the house itself, that

is, to make atonement for it, and in a sense to convert it into an altar. Seeing this blood, Jehovah, when He passed through to smite the Egyptians, would 'pass over the door,' so that it would 'not be granted . . . the destroyer to come in' unto their dwellings. . . . Thus, the term 'Passover,' or *Pasacha*, literally expresses the meaning and object of the ordinance.

"While all around the destroyer laid waste every Egyptian household, each company within the blood-sprinkled houses of Israel was engaged in the sacrificial meal. This consisted of the Paschal lamb, and 'unleavened bread with,' or rather 'upon, bitter herbs,' as if in that solemn hour of judgment and deliverance they were to have set before them as their proper meal the symbol of all the bitterness of Egypt, and upon it the sacrificial lamb and unleavened bread to sweeten and to make of it a festive supper. For everything here was of deepest meaning. The sacrificial lamb, whose sprinkled blood protected Israel, pointed to Him whose precious blood is the only safety of God's people; the hyssop (as in the cleansing of the leper, and of those polluted by death, and in Psalm 51:7) was the symbol of purification; and the unleavened bread that 'of sincerity and truth,' in the removal of the 'old leaven' which, as the symbol of corruption, pointed to 'the leaven of malice and wickedness.' More than that, the spiritual teaching extended even to details. The lamb was to be 'roast,' neither eaten 'raw,' or rather not properly cooked (as in the haste of leaving), nor yet 'sodden with water'—the latter because nothing of it was to pass into the water, nor the water to mingle with it, the lamb and the lamb alone being the food of the sacrificial company. For a similar reason it was to be roasted and served up whole—complete, without break or division, not a bone of it being broken, . . . just as not even a bone was broken of Him who died for us on the cross. . . . And this undividedness of the Lamb pointed not only to the entire surrender of the Lord Jesus, but also to our undivided union and communion in and with Him. . . . So also none of this lamb was to be kept for another meal, but that which had not been used must be burnt. Lastly, those who gathered around this meal were not only all

Israelites, but must all profess their faith in the coming deliverance; since they were to sit down to it with loins girded, with shoes on their feet and a staff in their hand, as it were, awaiting the signal of their redemption, and in readiness for departing from Egypt.

"A nobler spectacle of a people's faith can scarcely be conceived than when, on receiving these ordinances, 'the people bowed the head and worshipped' (Exodus 12:27). . . . Any attempt at description either of Israel's attitude or of the scenes witnessed when the Lord, passing through the land 'about midnight,' smote each firstborn from the only son of Pharaoh to the child of the maidservant and the captive, and even the firstborn of beasts, would only weaken the impression of the majestic silence of Scripture. Such things cannot be described—at least otherwise than by comparison with what is yet to follow. Suffice then, that it was a fit emblem of another 'midnight,' when the cry shall be heard: 'Behold, the Bridegroom cometh.'. . . In that midnight hour did Jehovah execute 'judgment against all the gods of Egypt,'. . . showing, as Calvin rightly remarks, how vain and false had been the worship of those who were now so powerless to help. That was also the night of Israel's birth as a nation: of their creation and adoption as the people of God. . . . Hence the very order of the year was now changed. The month of the Passover (*Abib*) became henceforth the first of the year. The Paschal supper was made a perpetual institution, with such new rules as to its future observance as would suit the people when settled in the land; . . . and its observance was to be followed by a 'feast of unleavened bread,' lasting for seven days, when all leaven should be purged out of their households. . . ." (Edersheim, *O.T.*, Vol. II, pages 78–82)

Every child could taste the difference in every morsel of food served during that week when all leaven was carefully purged out. And the Feast of Tabernacles also brought some special action when the whole family, from the youngest to the oldest, lived in booths, signifying not only a time of festival celebrating harvest, the *"feast of ingathering"* (Exodus 23:16), but to commemorate the leafy booths (succoth) in which they lodged

before they entered the desert. *"Ye shall dwell in booths seven days; all that are Israelites born shall dwell in booths: That your generations may know that I made the children of Israel to dwell in booths, when I brought them out of the land of Egypt: I am the LORD your God."* (Leviticus 23:42–43)

From William Smith's *A Dictionary of the Bible*: "The tents [or booths] of the wilderness furnished a home of freedom compared with the house of bondage out of which they had been brought. . . . the Israelite would be reminded with still greater edification of the perilous and toilsome march of his forefathers through the desert, when the nation seemed to be more immediately dependent on God for food, shelter and protection, while the completed harvest stored up for the coming winter set before him the benefits he had derived from the possession of the land flowing with milk and honey which had been of old promised to his race. . . ." (Vol. III, 1893 edition, pages 1423–24)

As a family carried out the detailed observance of these Providential events in the life of the nation the children began to take part. At some point in the service of the Paschal supper the youngest should rise and formally ask what was the meaning of all this service. *"And it shall come to pass, when your children shall say unto you, What mean ye by this service? That ye shall say, It is the sacrifice of the LORD's passover, who passed over the houses of the children of Israel in Egypt, when he smote the Egyptians, and delivered our houses. And the people bowed the head and worshipped."* (Exodus 12:26–27)

As the children asked, the father in each family would relate, in language which a young child could understand, the "whole national history of Israel, from the calling of Abraham down to the deliverance from Egypt and the giving of the law." The more fully this account was given and the better is was explained, the greater the impression it made upon the memory of each child present. So, from the time of babyhood were the young of each new generation made aware of the details of their unique history of liberty.

## HOME LIFE AND THE TEACHING OF THE LAW

Thus, the home life to which our Lord was accustomed was above all religious. There was private prayer, both morning and evening, and there was the "giving of thanks" both before and after each meal. In addition, of course, were the rituals which accompanied each act, the washings, the particular blessings, the separation of the sacred and the profane:

". . . The return of the Sabbath sanctified the week of labour. It was to be welcomed as a king, or with songs as a bridegroom; and each household observed it as a season of sacred rest and of joy. True, Rabbinism made all this a matter of mere externalism, converting it into an unbearable burden, by endless injunctions of what constituted work and of that which was supposed to produce joy, thereby utterly changing its sacred character. . . ." (Edersheim, *Sketches*, page 97)

Above all a devotion to the teaching of the Law characterized the homes of the children of Israel and

THE BOY CHRIST IN THE CARPENTER'S SHOP
by N. C. Wyeth, 1924. Used by Permission.

was the especial responsibility of the Fathers of Israel. There was however in this Galilean home of Jesus a deeper and more internal emphasis than that which had come to be associated with Rabbinism or traditionalism—the letter of the law which destroyed its spirit.

Josephus indicates that when Moses gave the children of Israel the laws and the constitution of government he believed that these laws were so very plain and easy that every father might be able to instruct his sons in it and every mother her daughters. It was important that the spirit of the Law be early communicated so that the individual became committed in his or her heart to a life of obedience to the Lord.

At the time of Jesus, however, the interpretation of the Law and the explicit directions for its observance outweighed the original purpose of keeping a people true to their covenant relationship to the Eternal God, of an overwhelming love for His path of godly living.

". . . From the outset, Jewish theology divided into two branches: the *Halakhah* and the *Haggadah*. The former (from *halakh*, to go) was, so to speak, the Rule of the Spiritual Road, and, when fixed, had even greater authority than the Scriptures of the Old Testament, since it explained and applied them. On the other hand, the *Haggadah** (from *nagad*, to tell) was only the personal saying of the teacher, more or less valuable according to his learning and popularity, or the authorities which he could quote in his support. Unlike the *Halakhah*, the *Haggadah* had no absolute authority, either as to doctrine practice, or exegesis.

". . . It is sadly characteristic, that practically, the main body of Jewish dogmatic and moral theology is really only *Haggadah*, and hence of no absolute authority. The *Halakhah* indicated with the most minute and painful punctiliousness every legal ordinance as to outward observances, and it explained every bearing of the Law of Moses. But beyond this it left the inner man, the spring of actions, untouched. What he was to believe

---

* Note: "The *Halakhah* might be described as the aprocryphal Pentateuch, the *Haggadah* as the apocryphal Prophets."

and what to feel, was chiefly matter of the Haggadah. Of course the laws of morality, and religion, as laid down in the Pentateuch, were fixed principles, but there was the greatest divergence and latitude in the explanation and application of many of them. . . . And here we may mark the fundamental distinction between the teaching of Jesus and Rabbinism. He left the *Halakhah* untouched, putting it, as it were, on one side, as something quite secondary, while He insisted as primary on that which to them was chiefly matter of Haggadah. And this rightly so, for, in His own words, 'Not that which goeth into the mouth defileth a man; but that which cometh out of the mouth,' since 'those things which proceed out of the mouth come forth from the heart, and they defile the man.' (Matthew 15:11, 18) The difference was one of fundamental principle, and not merely of development, form, or detail. The one developed the Law in its outward direction as ordinances and commandments; the other in its inward application as life and liberty. Thus Rabbinism occupied one pole—and the outcome of its tendency to pure externalism was the Halakhah, all that was internal and higher being merely Haggadic. The teaching of Jesus occupied the opposite pole. Its starting-point was the inner sanctuary in which God was known and worshipped, and it might well leave the Rabbinic Halakhoth aside, as not worth controversy, to be in the meantime 'done and observed,' in the firm assurance that, in the course of its development, the spirit would create its own appropriate forms, or, to use a New Testament figure, the new wine burst the old bottles. And, lastly, as closely connected with all this, and marking the climax of contrariety: Rabbinism started with demand of outward obedience and righteousness, and pointed to sonship as its goal; the Gospel started with the free gift of forgiveness through faith and of sonship, and pointed to obedience and righteousness as its goal. . . ." (Edersheim, *Messiah*, pages 8, 73–74)

## ORAL ABOVE WRITTEN LAW

One other aspect of "the tradition of the Elders" which the Child of Jesus was destined to transform was the emphasis of traditionalism to place the oral above the written law—the conviction that God's covenant was founded on the spoken rather than upon the written word. Edersheim explains:

". . . According to the Jewish view, God had given Moses on Mount Sinai alike the oral and the written Law, that is, the Law with all its interpretations and applications. From Exodus 20:1, it was inferred, that God had communicated to Moses the Bible, the Mishnah, and Talmud, and the Haggadah, even to that which scholars would in latest times propound. . . . In answer to the somewhat natural objection, why the Bible alone had been written, it was said that Moses had proposed to write down *all* the teaching entrusted to him, but the Almighty had refused, on account of the future subjection of Israel to the nations, who would take from them the written Law. Then the unwritten traditions would remain to separate between Israel and the Gentiles . . . ." (Edersheim, *Messiah*, page 69)

Thus, a body of repeated law and traditional ordinances, not always supported by Scripture, came to be elevated to the level of the Law of Moses recorded in the Pentateuch. That such an interpretation of law came to be destructive of the spirit of the Law itself, requiring 'teachers of the law' who were in actuality 'aristocrats' above 'the ordinary individual and the country-people,' was embodied in Jesus' denouncements of the scribes and Pharisees:

85

Then spake Jesus to the multitude, and to his disciples, Saying, The scribes
and the Pharisees sit in Moses' seat:

All therefore whatsoever they bid you observe, that observe and do; but do
not ye after their works: for they say, and do not.

For they bind heavy burdens and grievous to be borne, and lay them on
men's shoulders; but they themselves will not move them with one of
their fingers.

But all their works they do for to be seen of men: they make broad their phylacteries,* and enlarge** the borders of their garments,

And love the uppermost rooms at feasts, and the chief seats in the synagogues,

And greetings in the markets, and to be called of men, Rabbi, Rabbi.

But be not ye called Rabbi: for one is your Master, even Christ; and all ye
are brethren." (Matthew 23:1–8)

We know that our Lord found continual obstruction in His healing ministry from the Rabbinism of His time. He continually challenged the exchange of the external observation of the Law for the internal heart-attitude. His invective against the "blind guides" of the people found their full measure in chapter 23 of Matthew and He charged them with neglecting the original purpose of God's Law or Covenant with man: *"Woe unto you, scribes and Pharisees, hypocrites! for ye pay tithe of mint and anise and cummin, and have omitted the weightier matters of the law, judgment, mercy, and faith: these ought ye to have done, and not to leave the other undone."* (Matthew 23:23)

Ellicott comments on this particular passage:

*Ye pay tithe of mint and anise and cummin.*

"The language of Deuteronomy 12:17 seems to rec-ognise only corn, wine, and oil, among the produce of the earth, as subject to the law of tithes. The Pharisee, in his minute scrupulosity (based, it may be, on the more general language of Leviticus 27:30), made a point of gathering the tenth sprig of every garden herb, and presenting it to the priest. So far as this was done at the bidding of an imperfectly illumined conscience our Lord does not blame it. . . . What He did censure was the substitution of the lower for the higher. With the

---

* PHYLACTERIES. The Greek word (*phylacterion*) from which the English is derived signifies "safe-guard or preservative," and was probably applied under the idea that the phylacteries were charms or amulets against the evil eye or the power of evil spirits. This was the common meaning of the word in later Greek, and it is hardly likely to have risen among the Hellenis-tic Jews to the higher sense which has sometimes been ascribed to it, of being a means to keep men in mind of the obligations of the Law. Singularly enough, it is not used by the LXX trans-lators for the "frontlets" of Exodus 13:16; Deuteronomy 6:8; 11:18, . . .

"The latter reads: "Therefore shall ye lay up these my words in your heart and in—your soul, and bind them for a sign upon your hand, that they may be as frontlets before your eyes."

"The Hebrew word in common use from our Lord's time on-ward has been *tephillin,* or Prayers. The things so named were worn by well-nigh all Jews as soon as they became Children of the Law, *i.e.,* at thirteen. They consisted of a small box or cap-sule, "containing" small scrolls of parchment, on which were written the four passages in which frontlets are mentioned: Exo-

dus 13:2–16; Deuteronomy 6:4–9; 11:13–22. These were "written on four slips of vellum [or parchment] for the phylactery of the head, and on one for that of the arm [near the heart]. They were worn commonly during the act of prayer (hence the Hebrew name), and by those who made a show of perpetual devotion and study of the Law, during the whole day. The Pharisees, in their ostentatious show of piety, made either the box or the straps wider than the common size, and wore them as they walked to and fro in the streets, or prayed standing . . . that men might see and admire them." (See Ellicott, *N.T.,* Vol. 1, page 140.)

** Enlarging the borders of one's garments. This wearing of memorial fringes rested on Numbers 15:37,38: *"And the Lord spake unto Moses, saying, Speak unto the children of Israel, and bid them that they made them fringes in the borders of their garments throughout their generations, and that they put upon the fringe of the borders a ribband of blue."* The color of blue was "the colour symbolical of heaven." (Ellicott, *N.T.,* Vol. 1, page 140) three examples of the 'infinitely little' He contrasts the three ethical obligations that were infinitely great, 'judgment, mercy and faith.'" (*N.T.*, Vol. I, page 142)

It is inspiring to note the Providential Preparation of our Lord to free the Law from its essentially unscriptural deviations, and return it to its balance between the internal and external in the life of the individual. He was not subjected to nor brought up in the Rabbinic Schools of Judea. It was rather in Galilee with its more 'independent views' and 'milder' and more 'human' application of traditionalism where He abode. No wonder that the anger of the scribes and Pharisees against Him was directed not only at His just and loving treatment of all men, women and children, but at the fact that He was identified as a Galilean. Even the landscape of Judea was the embodiment of Jewish piety and asceticism—it was 'desolate, barren, and grey.' All this would favour "solitary thought and religious abstraction.

"It was quite otherwise in Galilee. The smiling landscape of Lower Galilee invited the easy labour of the agriculturist. Even the highlands of Upper Galilee . . . were not, like those of Judæa, sombre, lonely, enthusiasm-killing, but gloriously grand, free, fresh, and bracing. A more beautiful country—hill, dale, and lake —could scarcely be imagined than Galilee Proper . . . ." (Edersheim, *Messiah*, pages 155–56)

Once again we rejoice in the setting in which God the Father placed Jesus Christ for the preparation of His human and divine mission. Not only was Jesus as a Child nourished in a home which was tender, loving,

THE YOUTH OF JESUS by J. James Tissot

and devoted to the God of Israel. He was also in a home where the study of the Law, so precious to the children of a covenant nation, was mediated between Justice and Mercy, between a concern for the cultivation of the heart as well as compliance to rules and regulation.

## SUBJECTS OF STUDY IN JESUS' CHILDHOOD

In no nation in the history of the Old Testament were children so conscientiously educated as were the children of Israel. It was an education centered in religion and therefore all aspects and all subjects were related to knowledge of the Lord and His works, and to man's relationship to man in the light of God's principles.

That this education continued into the first century of our Lord's appearance—later denominated the first century of Christianity—is apparent in His own preparation and practice. Home life was full and rich in its significance to a Covenant people. The Old Testament Scriptures formed the basis of all education. Not only portions of Scripture—little rolls of parchment—but, as we infer in the home of Nazareth, ". . . a precious copy of the Sacred Volume in its entirety. At any rate, we know that from earliest childhood it must have formed the meat and drink of the God-Man. The words of the Lord, as recorded by St. Matthew, and St. Luke, . . . also imply that the Holy Scriptures which He read were in the original Hebrew, and that they were written in the square, or Assyrian, characters. . . . Indeed, as the Pharisees and Sadducees always appealed to the Scriptures in the original, Jesus could not have met them on any other ground, and it was this which gave such point to His frequent expostulations with them: 'Have ye not read?'" (Edersheim, *Messiah*, page 162)

The education of children was not confined to home although home was the center of all education. There was a great concern to establish schools and indeed it is reported that there were hundreds of schools in Jerusalem at the time of its destruction. Wherever there were one hundred and twenty families it was incumbent upon them to appoint a schoolmaster. School education began with the children ". . . gathered in Synogogues or in School-houses, . . . where at first they either stood, teachers and pupils alike, or else sat on the ground in a semicircle, facing the teacher. . . ." But there were also higher schools and Academies. ". . . [F]rom the teaching of the alphabet or of writing, onwards to the farthest limit of instruction in the most advanced Academies of the Rabbis, all is marked by extreme care, wisdom, accuracy, and a moral and religious purpose as the ultimate object. . . ." (Edersheim, *Messiah*, page 160)

The Bible was the exclusive textbook "up to ten years of age, . . . [f]rom ten to fifteen, the Mishnah, or traditional law; after that age, the student should enter on those theological discussions which occupied time and attention in the higher Academies of the Rabbis. . . . The study of the Bible commenced with that of the Book of Leviticus. . . . Thence it passed to other parts of the Pentateuch; then to the Prophets; and finally, to the hagiographa. . . ."* (Edersheim, *Messiah*, page 161)

The characteristics of an educated Israeli was ability to read fluently, to speak well, with special care in the choice of language and pronunciation, to have memorized "verses of Scripture, benedictions, wise sayings

etc.," as well as to know well and be able to repeat the history of Israel for all festive and memorial occasions. Memory was cherished and great importance laid to exact preservation of tradition. All subjects were merged with theology. The knowledge of the Law came to hold an exclusive importance. Heathen science and literature were prohibited.

But despite Rabbinical insistence upon literalism the schools were consistent with home life. The sacred obligation to preserve the innocence and purity of children, to keep out that which was coarse or vicious, ". . . to suppress all feelings of bitterness, even though real wrong had been done to one's parents; to punish all wrong-doing; . . ." and to be patient with pupils. For those who learned slowly it was "incumbent upon the teacher" to "make the lesson more plain. . . . excessive severity was to be avoided; . . ." (Edersheim, *Sketches*, pages 135–36)

What a contrast between the education of the children of Israel and that of the pagan world! The fact that the Book of Leviticus was the first book to be learned, characterizes the real purpose of their education. For the Book of Leviticus is the dedication of a people to "holiness." Leviticus describes God's "Holiness Code." It is explicit upon the ritual of holiness, the basis of "the removal of sin," or atonement. Thus, it points to "the eternal sacrifice" of Jesus Christ, and the New Covenant. As the Open Bible affirms: "The powerful message of Leviticus can be summarized by looking at the concepts of holiness, sacrifice, and atonement."

Ellicott's Introduction to Leviticus: "Design and Contents."

"The design of the Book has been aptly described as 'the spiritual statutebook of Israel as the congregation of God.' By the laws therein enacted, God designed

---

* HAGIOGRAPHY. "Sacred writings. The Jews divide the books of the Scriptures into three parts; the Law, which is contained in the five first books of the Old Testament; the Prophets, or Nevim; and the Cetuvim, or *writings*, by way of eminence. The latter class is called by the Greeks *Hagiographa*, comprehending the books of Psalms, Proverbs, Job, Daniel, Ezra, Nehemiah, Ruth, Esther, Chronicles, Canticles, Lamentations, and Ecclesiastes." (Webster 1828 *Dictionary*)

to train Israel as His peculiar people, to keep them from defilements, and to sanctify them for holy fellowship with their covenant Jehovah, who has deigned to erect His sanctuary in their midst. To effect this purpose enactments are in the first place laid down to regulate the access of the Israelites to the Divine Being as follows: The sacrifices which obtained from time immemorial are more minutely defined and systematised (chapter 1:1–chapter 7:38); the priesthood whose duty it is to offer these sacrifices are consecrated and installed (chapter 8:1–chapter 10:20); the uncleanness of animals (chapter 11:1–47); the impurities of men (chapter 12:1–chapter 15:33) which cause defilement and debar access to God are described; and, finally, the Day of Atonement is instituted, which is to expiate at the end of every year the neglect of any of the above-named regulations—(chapter 16:1–34), thus appropriately concluding the enactments which are designed to fit God's people for fellowship with Him. This group of laws is followed by sundry enactments which have for their object the holiness of the people in their every-day life, in their domestic relations, and in their intercourse with one another (chapter 17:1–chapter 20:27); the holiness of the priesthood, and their purity in their sacred ministrations (chapter 21:1–chapter 22:33); the sanctification of the festivals (chapter 23:1–chapter 24:12) and of the whole land (chapter 25:1–chapter 26:2); with directions about collateral questions arising from this part of legislation. The logical sequence of these different regulations, however, is not always apparent." (Ellicott, *O.T.*, Vol. 1, page 341–342)

Because of the silence of the Scriptures on Jesus' early years of education we are not able to know with certainty many things: ". . . whether the Child Jesus frequented the Synagogue School; who was His

SYNAGOGUE SCHOOL

teacher, and who those who sat beside Him on the ground, earnestly gazing on the face of Him Who repeated the sacrificial ordinances in the Book of Leviticus, that were all to be fulfilled in Him. . . . We do not even know quite certainly whether the school-system had, at that time, extended to far-off Nazareth; nor whether the order and method which have been described were universally observed at that time. In all probability, however, there was such a school in Nazareth, and, if so, the Child-Saviour would conform to the general practice of attendance. We may thus, still with the deepest reverence, think of Him as learning His earliest lesson from the Book of Leviticus. . . ." (Edersheim, *Messiah*, page 162)

ROMAN PERIOD WRITING
TABLET & STYLUS
Copyright:
R. Sheridan
Ancient Art & Architecture
Collection Ltd., UK
Used by Permission.

In the synagogue schools, the teacher wrote the letters of the Hebrew alphabet on a wax-covered wooden tablet, using a stylus. A typical tablet and stylus are shown here (most of the wax is worn off the tablet). The flattened end of the stylus was used for erasing. The children learned to recognize each letter by name, to call it aloud, and later to copy it on tablets of their own. . . . (*Jesus and His Times*, Readers' Digest, 1987, p. 152)

## CHRIST'S FIRST VISIT TO THE TEMPLE

The Gospel of Luke summarizes the Biblical Childhood of our Lord in a pious home in these words:

*"And the child grew, and waxed strong in spirit, filled with wisdom: and the grace of God was upon him."* (Luke 2:40)

The very next verses, Luke 2:41–42, bridge the years with the following statement:

*"Now his parents went to Jerusalem every year at the feast of the passover. And when he was twelve years old, they went up to Jerusalem after the custom of the feast." When he was twelve years old.*

"The stages of Jewish childhood were marked as follows:—At three the boy was weaned, and wore for the first time the fringed or tasselled garment prescribed by Numbers 15:38–41, and Deuteronomy 22:12. His education began, at first under his mother's care. At five he was to learn the Law, at first by extracts written on scrolls of the more important passages, . . . and by catechetical* teaching in school. At twelve he became more directly responsible for his obedience to the Law, and on the day when he attained the age of thirteen, put on for the first time the phylacteries which were worn at the recital of his daily prayer. . . . It was, therefore, in strict accordance with usage, with perhaps a slight anticipation of the actual day, that the 'child Jesus' should, at the age of twelve, have gone up with His parents to Jerusalem. If . . . the birth of our Lord coincided with the Paschal Season, . . . He may actually have completed His thirteenth year during the Feast; and so have become, in the fullest sense, one of the 'children of the Law,' bound to study it and know its meaning. This at least fits in with, and in fact explains, the narrative that follows. . . ." (Ellicott, *N.T.*, Vol. I, pages 257–58)

But before we can appreciate what this first visit to the Temple meant to our Lord, let us review the importance of the Temple to the Children of Israel.

## THE EXTERNAL TEMPLE

"Among the outward means by which the religion of Israel was preserved, one of the most important was the centralisation and localisation of its worship in Jerusalem. If to some the ordinances of the Old Testament may in this respect seem narrow and exclusive, it is at least doubtful, whether without such a provision Monotheism itself could have continued as a creed or a worship. In view of the state of the ancient world, and of the tendencies of Israel during the earlier stages of their history, the strictest isolation was necessary in order to preserve the religion of the Old Testament from that mixture with foreign elements which would speedily have proved fatal to its existence. And if one source of that danger had ceased after the seventy years' exile in Babylonia, the dispersion of the greater part of the nation among those whose manners and civilisation would necessarily influence them, rendered the continuance of this separation of as great importance as before. In this respect, even traditionalism had its mission and use, as a hedge around the Law to render its infringement or modification impossible.

"Wherever a Roman, a Greek, or an Asiatic might wander, he could take his gods with him, or find rites kindred to his own. It was far otherwise with the Jew. He had only one Temple, that in Jerusalem; only one God, Him Who had once throned there between the Cherubim, and Who was still King over Zion. That Temple was the only place where a God-appointed, pure priesthood could offer acceptable sacrifices, whether for forgiveness of sin, or for fellowship with God. Here, in the impenetrable gloom of the innermost sanctuary, which the High-Priest alone might enter once a year for most solemn expiation, had stood

---

\* CATECHETICAL: Relating to or consisting in asking questions and receiving answers, according to the ancient manner of teaching children. (Webster, 1828 *Dictionary*)

the Ark, the leader of the people into the Land of Promise, and the footstool on which the Shechinah had rested. From that golden altar rose the sweet cloud of incense, symbol of Israel's accepted prayers; that seven-branched candlestick shed its perpetual light, indicative of the brightness of God's Covenant Presence; on that table, as it were before the face of Jehovah, was laid, week by week, 'the Bread of the Face' ('shewbread'), a constant sacrificial meal which Israel offered unto God, and wherewith God in turn fed His chosen priesthood. On the great blood-sprinkled altar of sacrifice smoked the daily and festive burnt-offerings, brought by all Israel, and for all Israel, wherever

scattered; while the vast courts of the Temple were thronged not only by native Palestinians, but literally by 'Jews out of every nation under heaven.' Around this Temple gathered the sacred memories of the past; to it clung the yet brighter hopes of the future. The history of Israel and all their prospects were intertwined with their religion; so that it may be said that without their religion they had no history, and without their history no religion. Thus, history, patriotism, religion, and hope alike pointed to Jerusalem and the Temple as the centre of Israel's unity. . . ." (Edersheim, *Messiah*, page 3–4)

## JERUSALEM

" . . . As for Jerusalem, its situation was entirely unique. Pitched on a height of about 2,610 feet above the level of the sea, its climate was more healthy, equable, and temperate than that of any other part of the country. From the top of Mount Olivet an unrivalled view of the most interesting localities in the land might be obtained. To the east the eye would wander over the intervening plains to Jericho, mark the tortuous windings of Jordan, and the sullen grey of the Dead Sea, finally resting on Pisgah and the mountains of Moab and Ammon. To the south, you might see beyond 'the king's gardens,' as far as the grey tops of 'the hill-country of Judæa.' Westwards, the view would be arrested by the mountains of *Bether*, . . . whilst the haze in the distant horizon marked the line of the Great Sea. To the north, such well-known localities met the eye as Mizpeh, Gibeon, Ajalon, Michmash, Ramah, and Anathoth. But, above all, just at your feet, the Holy City would lie in all her magnificence, like 'a bride adorned for her husband.'. . .

" 'Beautiful for situation, the joy of the whole earth, is Mount Zion, on the sides of the north, the city of the Great King. . . . Walk about Zion, and go round about her: tell the towers thereof. Mark ye well her bulwarks, consider her palaces.' [Psalms 48:2,12,13] If this could be said of Jerusalem even in the humbler days of her na-

tive monarchy. . . , it was emphatically true at the time when Jesus 'beheld the city,' after Herod the Great had adorned it with his wonted splendour. As the pilgrim bands 'came up' from all parts of the country to the great feasts, they must have stood enthralled when its beauty first burst upon their gaze. . . . For Jerusalem was a city of palaces, and right royally enthroned as none other. Placed on an eminence higher than the immediate neighbourhood, it was cut off and isolated by deep valleys on all sides but one, giving it the appearance of an immense natural fortress. All around it, on three sides, like a natural fosse, ran the deep ravines of the Valley of Hinnom and of the Black Valley, or Kedron, which merged to the south of the city, descending in such steep declivity that where the two meet is 670 feet below the point whence each had started. . . . Only on the north-west was the city, as it were, bound to the mainland. And as if to give it yet more the character of a series of fortress-islands, a deep natural cleft—the Tyropoeon—ran south and north right through the middle of the city, then turned sharply westwards, separating Mount Zion from Mount Acra. Similarly, Acra was divided from Mount Moriah, and the latter again by an artificial valley from Bezetha, or the New Town. Sheer up from these encircling ravines rose the city of marble and cedar-covered palaces. Up

JERUSALEM IN THE TIME OF JESUS—SHOWING THE TEMPLE AND ANTONIO FORTRESS

that middle cleft, down in the valley, and along the slopes of the hills, crept the busy town, with its streets, markets, and bazaars. But alone, and isolated in its grandeur, stood the Temple Mount. Terrace upon terrace its courts rose, till, high above the city, within the enclosure of marble cloisters, cedar-roofed and richly ornamented, the Temple itself stood out a mass of snowy marble and of gold, glittering in the sunlight against the half-encircling green background of Olivet. In all his wanderings the Jew had not seen a city like his own Jerusalem. Not Antioch in Asia, not even imperial Rome herself, excelled it in architectural splendour. Nor has there been, either in ancient or modern times, a sacred building equal to the Temple, whether for situation or magnificence; nor yet have there been, festive throngs like those joyous hundreds of thousands who, with their hymns of praise, crowded towards the city on the eve of a Passover. . . .

"From whatever side the pilgrim might approach the city, the first impression must have been solemn and deep. But a special surprise awaited those who came, whether from Jericho or from Galilee, by the well-known road that led over the Mount of Olives. From the south, beyond royal Bethlehem—from the west, descending over the heights of Bethhoron—or from the north, journeying along the mountains of Ephraim, they would have seen the city first vaguely looming in the grey distance, till, gradually approaching, they had become familiar with its outlines. It was far otherwise from the east. A turn in the road, and the city, hitherto entirely hid from view, would burst upon them suddenly, closely, and to most marked advantage. It was by this road Jesus made His triumphal entry from Bethany on the week of His Passion. . . . Up from the 'house of dates' the broad, rough road wound round the shoulder of Olivet. Thither the wondering crowd from Bethany followed Him, and there the praising multitude from the city met Him. They had come up that same Olivet, so familiar to them all. For did it not seem almost to form part of the city itself, shutting it off like a screen from the desert land that descended beyond to Jordan and the Dead Sea? . . .

"From the Temple Mount to the western base of Olivet, it was not more than 100 or 200 yards straight across, though, of course, the distance to the summit was much greater, say about half a mile. By the nearest pathway it was only 918 yards from the city gate to the principal summit. . . . Olivet was always fresh and green, even in earliest spring or during parched summer—the coolest, the pleasantest, the most sheltered walk about Jerusalem. For across this road the Temple and its mountain flung their broad shadows, and luxuriant foliage spread a leafy canopy overhead. They were not gardens, in the ordinary Western sense, through which one passed, far less orchards; but something peculiar to those climes, where Nature everywhere strews with lavish hand her flowers, and makes her gardens—where the garden bursts into the orchard, and the orchard stretches into the field, till, high up, olive and fig mingle with the darker cypress and pine. The stony road up Olivet wound along terraces covered with olives, whose silver and dark green leaves rustled in the breeze. Here gigantic gnarled fig-trees twisted themselves out of rocky soil; there clusters of palms raised their knotty stems high up into waving plumed tufts, or spread, bush-like, from the ground, the rich-coloured fruit bursting in clusters from the pod. Then there were groves of myrtle, pines, tall, stately cypresses, and on the summit itself two gigantic cedars. To these shady retreats the inhabitants would often come from Jerusalem to take pleasure or to meditate, . . . Thither, also, Christ with His disciples often resorted.

"Coming from Bethany the city would be for some time completely hidden from view by the intervening ridge of Olivet. But a sudden turn of the road, where 'the descent of the Mount of Olives' begins, all at once a first glimpse of Jerusalem is caught, and that quite close at hand. True, the configuration of Olivet on the right would still hide the Temple and most part of the city; but across Ophel, the busy suburb of the priests, the eye might range to Mount Zion, and rapidly climb its height to where Herod's palace covered the site once occupied by that of David. A few intervening steps of descent, where the view of the city has again been lost, and the pilgrim would hurry on to that ledge of rock. What a panorama over which to roam with hungry eagerness! At one glance he would see before him the whole city—its valleys and hills, its walls and towers, its palaces and streets, and its magnificent Temple—almost like a vision from another world. There would be no difficulty in making out the general features of the scene. Altogether the city was only thirty-three stadia, or about four English miles, in circumference. Within this compass dwelt a population of 600,000 (according to Tacitus), but, according to the Jewish historian, amounting at the time of the Passover to between two and three millions. . . .

"In this hasty survey of the city no notice has been taken of the magnificent monuments and pillars erected in various parts of Jerusalem, nor of its synagogues, of which tradition fixes the number at from 460 to 480; nor of many public buildings; nor yet of such sacred spots as the Pool of Siloam, or that of Bethesda, on which memory loves to dwell. In sharp contrast to all this beauty and magnificence must have been the great walls and towers, and the detached forts, which guarded either the Temple or access to the various hills on which the city rose, . . .

"But to join the great crowd of worshippers we have to enter the city itself. Turning our back on Mount Zion, we now face eastwards to Mount Moriah. Though we look toward the four principle entrances to the Temple, yet what we see within those walls on the highest of the terraces is not the front but the back of the sanctuary. It is curious how tradition is here in the most palpable error in turning to the east in worship. The Holy Place itself faced eastwards, and was approached from the east; but most assuredly the ministering priests and the worshippers looked not towards the east, but towards the west. . . .

"The Temple plateau had been artificially levelled at immense labour and cost, and enlarged by gigantic substructures. The latter served also partly for the purpose of purification, as otherwise there might have been some dead body beneath, which, however great the distance from the surface, would, unless air had intervened, have, according to tradition, defiled the whole place above. As enlarged by Herod the Great, the Temple area occupied an elongated square of from 925 to 950 feet and upwards. . . . Roughly calculating it at about 1,000 feet, this would give an extent more than one-half greater than the length of St. Peter's at Rome, which measures 613 feet, and nearly double our own St. Paul's whose extreme length is 520½ feet. And then we must bear in mind that the Temple plateau was not merely about 1,000 feet in length, but a square of nearly 1,000 feet! It was not, however, in the centre of this square, but towards the north-west, that the Temple itself . . . was reached, its porch protruding, 'shoulder-like,' on either side—perhaps rising into two flanking towers—and covering the Holy and Most Holy Places. Thus must the 'golden fane' have been clearly visible from all parts; the smoke of its sacrifices slowly curling up against the blue Eastern sky, and the music of its services wafted across the busy city, while the sunlight glittered on its gilt roofs, or shone from its pavement of tesselated marble, or threw great shadows on Olivet behind. . . ." (Edersheim, *Temple*, pages 3–8; 12–15)

HEROD'S TEMPLE
From a Model

## WITHIN THE TEMPLE

Edersheim continues his description of how both the city and the Temple might have looked to our Lord when, as a youth of twelve or thirteen, he made his special pilgrimage. It is interesting too, to meditate on the great fact that while the view of Jerusalem must have been a great contrast to the humble Galilean village from which He had travelled, ". . . He who now looked upon it was not an ordinary Child. Nor are we, perhaps, mistaken in the idea that the sight of its grandeur would, as on another occasion, . . . awaken in Him not so much feelings of admiration, which might have been akin to those of pride, as of sadness, though He

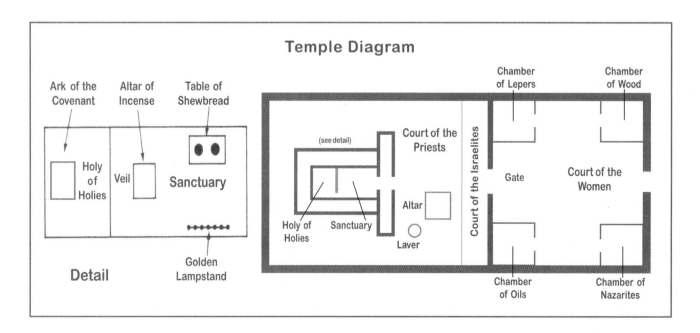

may as yet have been scarcely conscious of its deeper reason. . . . This, his first visit to its halls, seems also to have called out the first outspoken—and may we not infer, the first conscious—thought of that Temple as the House of His Father, and with it the first conscious impulse of his Mission and Being. Here also it would be the higher meaning, rather than the structure and appearance, of that Temple, that would absorb the mind. . . . Within the gates ran all around covered double colonnades, with here and there benches for those who resorted thither for prayer or for conference. The most magnificent of those was the southern, or twofold double colonnade, with a wide space between; the most venerable, the ancient 'Solomon's Porch,' or eastern colonnade. [See John 10:22,23.] . . . Passing along the eastern colonnade, or Solomon's Porch, we would, if the description of the Rabbis is trustworthy, have reached the Susa Gate, the carved representation of that city over the gateway reminding us of the *Eastern Dispersion*. . . .

"Passing out of these 'colonnades,' or 'porches,' you entered the 'Court of the Gentiles,' . . . This was called the *Chol*, or 'profane' place to which the Gentiles had access. Here must have been the market for the sale of sacrificial animals, the tables of the money-changers, and the places for the sale of other needful articles. . . ."

(See Jesus in this area of the Temple: Matthew 21:12–13; Mark 11:15–17; Luke 19:45–46; John 2:13–21.)

"Advancing within this Court, you reached a low breast-wall (the *Soreg*), which marked the space beyond which no Gentile, nor Levitically unclean person, might proceed—tablets, bearing inscriptions to that effect, warning them off. Thirteen openings admitted into the inner part of the Court. Thence fourteen steps led up to the *Chel* or Terrace, which was bounded by the wall of the Temple-buildings in the stricter sense. A flight of steps led up to the massive, splendid gates. The two on the west side seem to have been of no importance, so far as the worshippers were concerned, and probably intended for the use of workmen. North and south were four gates. . . . But the most splendid gate was that to the east, termed 'the Beautiful.'. . . (See Acts 3:2,10.)

"Entering by the latter, you came into the Court of the Women, so called because the women occupied it in two elevated and separated galleries, which, however, filled only part of the Court. Fifteen steps led up to the Upper Court, which was bounded by a wall, and where was the celebrated Nicanor Gate, covered with Corinthian brass. Here the Levites, who conducted the musical part of the service, were placed. In the Court of the Women were the Treasury and the thirteen 'Trumpets,' while at each corner were chambers or halls, destined for various purposes. Similarly, beyond the fifteen steps, there were repositories for the musical instruments. The Upper Court was divided into two parts by a boundary—the narrow part forming the Court of Israel, and the wider that of the Priests, in which were the great Altar and the Laver.

"The Sanctuary itself was on a higher terrace than the Court of the Priests. Twelve steps led up to its Porch, which extended beyond it on either side (north and south). Here, in separate chambers, all that was necessary for the sacrificial service was kept. On two marble tables near the entrance the old shewbread which was taken out, and the new that was brought in, were respectively placed. The Porch was adorned by votive presents, conspicuous among them a massive golden vine. A two-leaved gate opened into the Sanctuary itself, which was divided into two parts. The *Holy Place* had the Golden Candlestick (south), the Table of Shewbread (north), and the Golden Altar of Incense between them. A heavy double veil concealed the entrance to the *Most Holy Place*, which in the second Temple was empty, nothing being there but the piece of rock, called the *Ebhen Shethiyah*, or Foundation Stone, which, according to tradition, covered the mouth of the pit, and on which, it was thought, the world was founded. Nor does all this convey an adequate idea of the vastness of the Temple-buildings. For all around the Sanctuary and each of the Courts were various chambers and out-buildings, which served different purposes connected with the Services of the Temple. . . ." (Edersheim, *Messiah*, pages 168–70)

## JESUS "SITTING IN THE MIDST OF THE DOCTORS"

The gospel narrative indicates that this first visit of our Lord to the Temple was to be marked by a number of significant happenings. Up to this time in the Life of our Lord, as the Child Jesus, He had passed his first twelve or thirteen years wholly within the sight of His earthly guardians. But on this occasion the quiet Child seemed to pass into young Manhood and to separate Himself for just a brief moment from His human relationships into a threshold vision of His mission.

We know that Jesus, Joseph and Mary had traveled to Jerusalem in a large company of kinsfolk and friends. Luke reports the following:

*"Now his parents went to Jerusalem every year at the feast of the passover. And when he was twelve years old, they went up to Jerusalem after the custom of the feast. And when they had fulfilled the days, as they returned, the child Jesus tarried behind in Jerusalem; and Joseph and his mother knew not of it.*

*But they, supposing him to have been in the company, went a day's journey; and they sought him among their kinsfolk and acquaintance. And when they found him not, they turned back again to Jerusalem, seeking him. And it came to pass, that after three days they found him in the temple, sitting in the midst of the doctors, both hearing them, and asking them questions. And all that heard him were astonished at his understanding and answers.*

*And when they saw him, they were amazed: and his mother said unto him, Son, why hast thou thus dealt with us? behold, thy father and I have sought thee sorrowing. And he said unto them, How is it that ye sought me? wist ye not that I must be about my Father's business? And they understood not the saying which he spake unto them."* (Luke 2:41–50)

Detail, CHRIST TEACHING IN THE TEMPLE by Carl Bloch, 1834–1890
Frederiksborg Museet, Hilleroed DK, US agent HOPE GALLERY. Used by permission.

## "THE AWAKENING OF THE CHRIST-CONSCIOUSNESS"

In this first visit to the Temple, His Father's House, the most visible evidence of the One God of Israel, came, what Dr. Edersheim calls "the awakening of the Christ-consciousness." In his words Jesus "felt the strong and irresistible impulse—that Divine necessity of His Being—to be 'about His Father's business.'" When His parents found Him sitting among the Doctors, "both hearing them, and asking them questions," He may have been discussing the Paschal solemnities which were even now being celebrated. And the young Jesus, He who would be the Great Paschal Offering, as *"the Lamb of God, which taketh away the sin of the world,"* might even then have been contemplating the deeper meaning of that sacrifice for mankind.

The visible lambs offered for slaughter, the visible Temple with its magnificence and its religious significance, was to be replaced by a Greater Offering—One in which Propitiation and Sacrifice would bring closer the Infinite All-Loving and Forgiving Father. Mercifully, we believe only a glimpse of His Great Mission appeared to our Lord at this time. And for Mary, too,

only a dim awareness permeated her consciousness as both she and Joseph urged the Youth to come home. Yet, like other Divine Moments in her life, Mary knew that the contrast between the quiet boy in their home, and His presence and profession in the Temple had meaning. As Edersheim comments: "She was learning to spell out the word Messiah, as each of 'those matters' taught her one fresh letter in it, and she looked at them all in the light of the Nazareth-Sun." (Edersheim, *Messiah*, page 173)

*"And he went down with them, and came to Nazareth, and was subject unto them: but his mother kept all these sayings in her heart. And Jesus increased in wisdom and stature, and in favour with God and man."* (Luke 2:51–52)

It would be seventeen, almost eighteen years before Jesus our Lord would begin to perform His first purging of the Temple. He who had glimpsed His Messianic Mission had many a year still to live and prepare Himself as quiet uneventful days and deeds unfolded —pearls of Providential preparation—held in the Hand of God.

## BIBLICAL CHILDHOOD AND MINISTRY OF THE FORERUNNER

John the Baptist stands at the climax of both the Old and New Testament as "a saint signally honored of God." Through his miraculous birth, foretold by the Angel Gabriel, by his name, John, assigned by God, he was indeed born of God's especial favour, to be the harbinger of Grace. Furthermore, as foretold by the Angel, *". . . He shall be great in the sight of the Lord, and shall drink neither wine nor strong drink; and he shall be filled with the Holy Ghost, even from his mother's womb. And many of the children of Israel shall he turn to the Lord their God. And he shall go before him in the spirit and power of Elias, to turn the hearts of the fathers to the children, and the disobedient to the wisdom of the just; to make ready a people prepared for the Lord."* (Luke 1:15–17)

Scripture has little to report on John's childhood

and preparation for his ministry. It is probable that his early years were spent at home learning from both his father, Zacharias, and his mother, Elizabeth, in their appointed roles.

The last verse of the first chapter of Luke records: *"And the child grew, and waxed strong in spirit, and was in the deserts till the day of his shewing unto Israel."* (Luke 1:80)

Matthew Henry's commentary on this passage:

"Of his *eminence* as to the *inward man*: The *child grew* in the capacities of his mind, much more than other children; so that he *waxed strong in his spirit*, had a strong judgment and strong resolution. Reason and conscience (both which are the candle of the Lord) were so strong in him that he had the inferior faculties of appetite and passion in complete subjection betimes. By this it appeared that he was betimes *filled with the Holy Ghost*; for those that are strong in the Lord are *strong in spirit.*

"Of his *obscurity* as to the *outward man: He was in the deserts*; not that he lived a hermit, cut off from the society of men. No, we have reason to think that he went up to Jerusalem at the *feasts*, and frequented the synagogues on the sabbath day, but his constant residence was in some of those scattered houses that were in the wilderness of Zuph or Maon, which we read of in the story of David. There he spent most of his time, in contemplation and devotion, and had not his education in the schools, or at the feet of the rabbin. . . ." (Henry, Vol. V, pages 595–96)

Ellicott records that he had the usual Jewish education, and that "the observance of the Nazarite vow, and the death of his parents while he was comparatively young" sent him to the "deserts that surrounded the western shores of the Dead Sea" into "study and meditation given to the Law and the Prophets" waiting for the time of his calling and showing to Israel.

The Angel Gabriel's message to Zacharias had indicated that the Forerunner should have a ministry like that of Elijah. Edersheim makes a comparison of the ministry of Elijah and John which explains why the Baptist had to fulfill both the requirements of an Old Testament Prophet and that of the Forerunner of the

JOHN BEFORE HEROD

New Testament of Grace whereby the means of repentance was embodied in an inward and an outward obedience to the God's requirements of the Law.

Like Elijah, John first bore witness to a "society secure, prosperous, and luxurious, yet in imminent danger of perishing from hidden festering disease." He also had to testify to a religious community which presented a picture of moral perversion, yet "contained the germs of a possible regeneration." God's judgment was presented by both Prophets as 'threatening' unless there was a change of hearts. Both presented a stark contrast to the materialism and hopelessness of their times. John came suddenly out of the wilderness of Judæa, as Elijah came from the wilds of Gilead; John bore the same strange ascetic appearance as his predecessor." (Edersheim, *Messiah*, page 177)

In the book of Matthew we see the most graphic portrait of John the Baptist:

*"In those days came John the Baptist, preaching in the wilderness of Judæa, And saying, Repent ye: for the kingdom of heaven is at hand. For this is he that was spoken of by the prophet Esaias, saying, The voice of one crying in the wilderness, Prepare ye the way of the Lord, make his paths straight. And the same John had his raiment of camel's hair, and a leathern girdle about his loins; and his meat was locusts and wild honey."* (Matthew 3:1–4)

Ellicott comments:

*His raiment of camel's hair.*
"The dress was probably deliberately adopted by the Baptist as reviving the outward appearance of Elijah, who was a 'hairy man, and girt with a girdle of leather' (II Kings 1:8); and the 'rough garment,' that had been characteristic of the prophet's life even at a later period (Zechariah 8:4), as contrasted with the 'long garments' of the Pharisees (Mark 12:38), and the 'gorgeous apparel' of the scribes who attached themselves to the court of Herod (Luke 7:35). The Nazarite vow of Luke 1:15 probably involved long and shaggy hair as well.

*Locusts and wild honey.*

"Locusts were among the articles of food permitted by the Law (Leviticus 11:21), and were and are still used by the poor in Palestine and Syria. They are commonly salted and dried, and may be cooked in various ways, pounded, or fried in butter, and they taste like shrimps. . . . The 'wild honey' was that found in the hollows of trees (as in the history of Jonathan, I Samuel 14:25), or in the 'rocks' (Deuteronomy 32:13; Psalm 81:16). Stress is laid on the simplicity of the Baptist's fare, requiring no skill or appliances, the food of the poorest wanderer in the wilderness, presenting a marked contrast to the luxury of the dwellers in towns. . . ." (Ellicott, *N.T.*, Vol. I, page 10)

The Gospel of Luke records when the time of 'John's showing unto Israel' came:

*"Now in the fifteenth year of the reign of Tiberius Cæsar, Pontius Pilate being governor of Judæa, and Herod being tetrarch of Galilee, . . . Annas and Caiaphas being the high priests, the word of God came unto John the son of Zacharias in the wilderness. And he came into all the country about Jordan, preaching the baptism of repentance for the remission of sins; As it is written in the words of Esaias the prophet, saying, The voice of one crying in the wilderness, Prepare ye the way of the Lord, make his paths straight."* (Luke 3:1-4)

Matthew Henry comments:

"The date of the beginning of John's baptism" was "by the reign of the Roman emperor; . . . The people of the Jews, after a long struggle, were of late made a province of the empire, and were under the dominion of this Tiberius; . . . The lawgiver was now departed from between Judah's feet; and, as an evidence of that, their public acts are dated by the reign of the Roman emperor, and therefore now Shiloh must come.

"It is dated by the governments of the viceroys that ruled in the several parts of the Holy Land under the Roman emperor, which was another badge of their servitude, . . ." and "By the government of the Jews among themselves, to show that they were a corrupt people, and that therefore it was time that the Messiah should come, to reform them, . . ." (Henry, Vol. V, pages 610–11)

Edersheim discusses the internal and external responses of the "'Voice crying in the wilderness: Repent! for the Kingdom of Heaven is at hand,'. . .

"[It] awakened echoes throughout the land, and brought from city, village, and hamlet strangest hearers. For once, every distinction was levelled. Pharisee and Sadducee, outcast, publican and semi-heathen soldier, met here as on common ground. Their bond of union was the common 'hope of Israel'—the only hope that remained: that of 'the Kingdom.' The long winter of disappointment had not destroyed, nor the storms of suffering swept away, nor yet could any plant of spurious growth overshadow, what had struck its roots so deep in the soil of Israel's heart.

"That Kingdom had been the last word of the Old Testament. As the thoughtful Israelite, whether Eastern or Western, viewed even the central part of his worship in sacrifices, and remembered that his own Scriptures had spoken to them in terms which pointed to something beyond their offering. . . , he must have felt that 'the blood of bulls and of goats, and the ashes of an heifer sprinkling the unclean,' could only 'sanctify to the purifying of the flesh;' that, indeed, the whole body of ceremonial and ritual ordinances 'could not make him that did the service perfect as pertaining to the conscience.'. . .

"It was otherwise with the thought of the Kingdom. Each successive link in the chain of prophecy bound Israel anew to this hope, and each seemed only more firmly welded than the other. . . . So closely has it been intertwined with the very life of the nation, that, to all believing Israelites, this hope has through the long night of ages, been like that eternal lamp which burns in the darkness of Synagogue, in front of the heavy veil that shrines the Sanctuary, which holds and conceals the precious rolls of the Law and the Prophets." (Edersheim, *Messiah*, pages 191–92)

John's message of repentance was to all walks of life, that the external activities, reflect an internal change of heart. Luke records:

*"Then said he to the multitude that came forth to be baptized of him, O generation of vipers, who hath warned you to flee from the wrath to come? Bring forth therefore fruits worthy of repentance, and begin not to say within yourselves, We have Abraham to our father: for I say unto you, That God is able of these stones to raise up children unto Abraham. And now also the axe*

SAINT JOHN THE BAPTIST AND THE PHARISEES by J. James Tissot

*is laid unto the root of the trees: every tree therefore which bringeth not forth good fruit is hewn down, and cast into the fire. And the people asked him, saying, What shall we do then? He answered and saith unto them, He that hath two coats, let him impart to him that hath none; and he that hath meat let him do likewise. Then came also publicans to be baptized, and said unto him, Master, what shall we do? And he said unto them, Exact no more than that which is appointed you. And the soldiers likewise demanded of him, saying, And what shall we do? And he said unto them, Do violence to no man, neither accuse any falsely; and be content with your wages."* (Luke 3:7–14)

Matthew Henry comments:

"The particular instructions he gave to the several sorts of persons, that enquired of him concerning their duty: the *people*, the *publicans*, and the *soldiers*. Some

of the Pharisees and Sadducees came to his baptism; but we do not find them asking, *What shall we do?* They thought they knew what they had to do as well as he could tell them, or were determined to do what they pleased, whatever he told them. But the *people*, the *publicans*, and the *soldiers*, who knew that they had done amiss, and that they ought to do better, and were conscious to themselves of great ignorance and unacquaintedness with the divine law, were particularly inquisitive: *What shall we do?* . . .

"He tells the *people* their duty, and that is to be charitable . . . : *He that has two coats*, and consequently, one to spare, let him *give*, or *lend* at least, *to him that has none*, to keep him warm. . . . The gospel requires *mercy*, and not sacrifice; and the design of it is to engage us to do all the good we can. *Food and raiment* are the two supports of life; he that hath *meat* to spare, let him give to him that is destitute of *daily food*, as well as he that hath clothes to spare: what we have we are but stewards of, and must use it accordingly, as our Master directs.

"He tells the *publicans* their duty, the collectors of the emperor's revenue: . . . *Exact no more than that which is appointed you.* They must do justice between the government and the merchant, and not oppress the people in levying the taxes, nor any way make them heavier or more burdensome than the law had made them. . . . 'No, keep to your *book of rates*, and reckon it enough that you collect for Cæsar the things that are Cæsar's, and do not enrich yourselves by taking more.' The public revenues must be applied to the public service, and not to gratify the avarice of private persons. Observe, He does not direct the publicans to quit their places, and to go no more to the receipt of custom; the employment is in itself lawful and necessary, but let them be just and honest in it.

"He tells the *soldiers* their duty. . . . Some think that these soldiers were of the Jewish nation and religion: others think that they were Romans; for it was not likely either that the Jews would serve the Romans or that the Romans would trust the Jews in their garrisons in their own nation; and then it is an early instance of Gentiles embracing the gospel and submitting to it. Military men seldom seem inclined to religion; yet these submitted even to the Baptist's strict profession, and desired to receive the *word of command* from him: *What must we do?* . . . John does not bid them lay down their arms, and desert the service, but cautions them against the sins that the soldiers were commonly guilty of; for this is fruit meet for repentance, *to keep ourselves from our iniquity*. They must not be injurious to *the people* among whom they were quartered, and over whom indeed they were set. '*Do violence to no man*. Your business is to keep the peace, and prevent men's doing violence to one another; but do not you *do violence* to any. Shake no man,' (so the word signifies); 'do not put people into fear; for the sword of war, as well as that of justice, is to be a terror only to evil doers, but a protection to those that do well. Be not rude in your quarters; force not money from people by frightening them. Shed not the blood of war in peace; offer no incivility either to man or woman, nor have any hand in the barbarous devastations that armies sometimes make.'

"Nor must they *accuse any falsely* to the government, thereby to make themselves formidable and get bribes.

"They must not be injurious to their *fellow-soldiers*; for some think that caution, not to *accuse falsely*, has special reference to them: 'Be not forward to complain one of another to your superiour officers, that you may be revenged on those whom you have a pique against, or undermine those above you, and get into their places.' . . .

"'*Be content with your wages*. While you have what you agreed for, do not murmur that it is not more.' It is discontent with what they have that makes men oppressive and injurious; that they never think they have enough themselves will not scruple at any the most irregular practices to make it more, by defrauding others. It is a rule to all servants that they *be content with their wages*; for they that indulge themselves in discontents, expose themselves to many temptations, and it is wisdom to make the best of that which is."

It is now "drawing near to the appearance of our Lord Jesus [Christ] . . . ; the Sun will not be long after the morning-star." (Henry, Vol. V, pages 613–14)

John makes one more qualification between his own ministry and that of our Lord:

"*I indeed baptize you with water unto repentance: but he that cometh after me is mightier than I, whose shoes I am not worthy to bear: he shall baptize you with the Holy Ghost, and with fire: Whose fan is in his hand, and he will throughly purge his floor, and gather his wheat into the garner; but he will burn up the chaff with unquenchable fire.*" (Matthew 3:11–12)

## THE BAPTISM OF JESUS CHRIST

Each of the four Gospels gives the account of our Lord's baptism in the River Jordan.

Matthew 3:13–17

"*Then cometh Jesus from Galilee to Jordan unto John, to be baptized of him. But John forbad him, saying, I have need to be baptized of thee, and comest thou to me? And Jesus answering said unto him, Suffer it to be so now: for thus it becometh us to fulfill all righteousness. Then he suffered him. And Jesus, when he was bap-*

*tized, went up straightway out of the water: and, lo, the heavens were opened unto him, and he saw the Spirit of God descending like a dove, and lighting upon him. And lo a voice from heaven, saying, This is my beloved Son, in whom I am well pleased.*"

Mark 1:9–11

"*And it came to pass in those days, that Jesus came from Nazareth of Galilee, and was baptized of John in Jordan. And straightway coming up out of the water, he*

CHRIST COMING UP OUT OF THE JORDAN by Benjamin West, P.R.A., English, 1738–1820

From the Bob Jones University Collection. Used by permission.

*saw the heavens opened, and the Spirit like a dove descending upon him: And there came a voice from heaven, saying, Thou art my beloved Son, in whom I am well pleased."*

Luke 3:21–22

*"Now when all the people were baptized, it came to pass, that Jesus also being baptized, and praying, the heaven was opened. And the Holy Ghost descended in a bodily shape like a dove upon him, and a voice came from heaven, which said, Thou art my beloved Son; in thee I am well pleased."*

John 1:29–34

*"The next day John seeth Jesus coming unto him, and saith, Behold the Lamb of God, which taketh away the sin of the world. This is he of whom I said, After me cometh a man which is preferred before me: for he was before me. And I knew him not: but that he should be made manifest to Israel, therefore am I come baptizing with water.*

*"And John bare record, saying, I saw the Spirit descending from heaven like a dove, and it abode upon him. And I knew him not: but that he sent me to baptize with water, the same said unto me, Upon whom thou shalt see the Spirit descending, and remaining on him, the same is he which baptizeth with the Holy Ghost. And I saw, and bare record that this is the Son of God."*

It was now time for John the Baptist to recognize our Lord Jesus Christ for a second time. We remember that as a babe of five months in the womb of his mother Elizabeth, he had leaped when the Virgin Mary came to visit her cousin. Edersheim recounts this meeting of the opening step in the ministry of Jesus:

"When tidings of John's Baptism reached His home, there could be no haste on His part. Even with knowledge of all that concerned John's relation to Him, there was in the 'fulfillment of all righteousness' quiet waiting. The one question with Him was, as He afterwards put it: 'The Baptism of John, whence was

it? from heaven, or of men?' (Matthew 21:25). That question once answered, there could no longer be doubt nor hesitation. He went—not for any ulterior purpose, nor from any other motive than that it *was of God*. He went voluntarily, because it was such—and because 'it became Him' in so doing 'to fulfill all righteousness.'... But as, on His first visit to the Temple, this consciousness about His Life-business came to Him in His Father's House, ripening slowly and fully those long years of quiet submission and growing wisdom and grace at Nazareth, so as His Baptism, with the accompanying descent of the Holy Ghost, His abiding in Him, and the heard testimony from His Father, the knowledge came to Him, and, in and with . . . that knowledge, the qualification for the business of His Father's House. In that hour He learned the *when*, and in part the *how*, of His Life-business; the latter to be still farther, and from another aspect, seen in the wilderness, then in His life, in His suffering, and, finally, in His death. . . . But the first step to all was His voluntary *descent* to Jordan, and in it the fulfilling of all righteousness. His previous life had been that of the Perfect Ideal Israelite—believing, unquestioning, submissive—in preparation for that which, in His thirteenth year, he had learned as its business. The Baptism of Christ was the last act of His private life; and, emerging from its waters in prayer, He learned: *when* His business was to commence, and *how* it would be done." (Edersheim, *Messiah*, pages 194–95)

It is significant the place where Jesus was baptized of John.

*"In Bethabara beyond Jordan,* . . . Bethabara signifies the *house of passage;* some think it was the very place where Israel passed over Jordan into the land promised under the conduct of Joshua; there was opened the way into the gospel state by Jesus Christ. It was at a great *distance* from Jerusalem beyond Jordan; probably because what he did *there* would be least offensive to the government. . . ; it was sad that Jerusalem should put so far from her the things that belonged to *her peace. . . ."* (Henry, Vol. V, page 860)

## THE MARTYRDOM OF JOHN THE BAPTIST

"With the Baptism of Jesus, John's more especial office ceased. The King had come to His Kingdom. The function of the herald was discharged. It was this that John had with singular humility and self-renunciation announced beforehand: 'He must increase, but I must decrease.'

"John, however, still continued to present himself to his countrymen in the capacity of witness to Jesus. . . . But shortly after he had given his testimony to the Messiah, John's public ministry was brought to a close. He had at the beginning of it condemned the hyprocrisy and worldliness of the Pharisees and Sadducees, and he now had occasion to denounce the lust of a king. In daring disregard of the Divine laws, Herod Antipas had taken to himself the wife of his brother Philip; and when John reproved him for this, as well as for other sins (Luke 3:19), Herod cast him into prison. The place of his confinement was the castle of Machaerus—a fortress on the eastern shore of the Dead Sea. It was here that reports reached him of the miracles which our Lord was working in Judea—miracles which, doubtless, were to John's mind but the confirmation of what he expected to hear as to the establishment of the Messiah's Kingdom. But if Christ's Kingdom were indeed established, it was the duty of John's own disciples no less than of all others to acknowledge it. They, however, would naturally cling to their own master, and be slow to transfer their allegiance to another. With a view therefore of overcoming their scruples, John sent two of them to Jesus Himself to ask the question, *'Art Thou He that should come?'* They were answered not by words, but by a series of miracles wrought before their eyes—the very miracles which prophecy had specified as the distinguishing credential of the Messiah (Isaiah 35:5,6; Isaiah 61:1); and while Jesus bade the two messengers carry back to John as His only answer the report of what they had seen and heard, He took occasion to guard the multitude who surrounded Him, against supposing that the Baptist himself was shaken in mind, by a direct appeal to their own knowledge of his life and character. Well might they be appealed to as witnesses that the stern prophet of the wilderness was no waverer, bending to every breeze, like the reeds on the banks of the Jordan. Proof abundant had they that John was no worldling with a heart set upon rich clothing and dainty fare—the luxuries of a king's court —and they must have been ready to acknowledge that one so inured to a life of hardness and privation was not likely to be affected by the ordinary terrors of a prison. But our Lord not only vindicates His forerunner from any suspicion of inconstancy, He goes on to proclaim him a prophet, and more than a prophet; nay, inferior to none born of woman, though in respect to spiritual privileges behind the least of those who were to be born of the Spirit and admitted into the fellowship of Christ's Body (Matthew 11:11).

"Jesus further proceeds to declare that John was, according to the true meaning of the prophecy, the Elijah of the new covenant, foretold by Malachi (3:4). The event indeed proved that John was to Herod what Elijah had been to Ahab, and a prison was deemed too light a punishment for his boldness in asserting God's Law before the face of a king and a queen. Nothing but the death of the Baptist would satisfy the resentment of Herodias. . . .

Salome, prompted by her abandoned mother, demanded the head of John the Baptist. The promise had been given in the hearing of his distinguished guests, and so Herod, though loth to be made the instrument of so bloody a work, gave instructions to an officer of his guard, who went and executed John in the  prison, and his head was brought to feast the eyes of the adulteress whose sins he had denounced.

"Thus was John added to that glorious army of martyrs who have suffered for righteousness' sake. His death is supposed to have occurred just before the third Passover, in the course of the Lord's ministry....

"The brief history of John's life is marked throughout with the characteristic graces of self-denial, humility, and holy courage. So great indeed was his abstinence that worldly men considered him possessed. 'John came neither eating nor drinking, and they said he hath a devil.' His humility was such that he had again and again to disavow the character, and decline the honours which an admiring multitude almost forced upon him. To their questions he answered plainly, he was not the Christ, nor the Elijah of whom they were thinking, nor one of their old Prophets. He was no one—a voice merely—the Voice of God calling His people to repentance in preparation for the coming of Him whose shoe latchet he was not worthy to unloose.

"For his boldness in speaking truth, he went a willing victim to prison and to death. . . ." (Smith, *Dictionary*, Vol. I, Part II, pages 1738–39)

## CHRIST THE VICTOR OVER SATAN

The synoptic Gospels of Matthew, Mark and Luke all record that Christ's first act following His baptism by John, was to be '*led*' or '*driven*,' by the Holy Spirit '*into the wilderness, to be tempted of the devil*.' It would seem that having been announced by the Holy Spirit as '*my beloved Son, in whom I am well pleased*,' Jesus must now qualify Himself before man as their only hope of conquest against the arch foe of mankind. Matthew Henry, 'the prince of Bible commentators,' puts it thus:

"We have here the story of a famous duel fought hand to hand, between Michael and the dragon, the Seed of the woman and the seed of the serpent, nay, the serpent himself; in which the seed of the woman suffers, being *tempted*, and so has his heel bruised; but the serpent is quite baffled in his temptations, and so has his head broken; and our Lord Jesus comes off a Conqueror, and so secures not only comfort, but conquest at last, to all his faithful followers. . . .

"The place where it was; *in the wilderness*; probably in the great wilderness of *Sinai*, where Moses and Elijah *fasted forty days*, for no part of the *wilderness* of Judea was so abandoned to wild beasts as this is said to have been, Mark 1:13. . . .

"He was directed to the combat; he did not wilfully thrust himself upon it, but he *was led up of the Spirit to be tempted of the Devil*. The Spirit that *descended upon him like a dove* made him meek, and yet made him bold. . . .

"Christ *was led to be tempted of the Devil*, and of him only. Others are tempted, *when they are drawn aside of their own lust and enticed* (James 1:15); the Devil takes hold of that handle, and ploughs with that heifer: but our Lord Jesus had no corrupt nature, and therefore he was led securely, without any fear or trembling, as a champion into the field, *to be tempted* purely by *the Devil*.

"Now Christ's temptation is, . . . An instance of his own condescension and humiliation. Temptations are *fiery, darts, thorns in the flesh, buffetings, siftings, wrestlings, combats*, all which denote hardship and suffering; *therefore* Christ submitted to them, because he would humble himself, *in all things to be made like unto his brethren*. . . .

"He was dieted for the combat, as wrestlers, who are *temperate in all things* (I Corinthians 9:25); but Christ beyond any other, for he *fasted forty days and forty nights*, in compliance with the type and example of Moses the great lawgiver, and of Elias, the great reformer, of the Old Testament. John the Baptist came as Elias, in those things that were moral, but not in such things as were miraculous (John 10:41); that honour was reserved for Christ. Christ needed not to fast for mortification (he had no corrupt desires to be subdued); yet he *fasted*, . . . That herein he might humble himself, . . . That he might give Satan both occasion and advantage against him; and so make his victory over him the more illustrious. . . .

"The temptations themselves. That which Satan aimed at, in all his temptations, was, to bring him to *sin against God*, and so to render him for ever incapable of being a Sacrifice for the sins of others. . . . To

105

despair of his Father's goodness. . . . To presume upon his Father's power. . . . To alienate his Father's honour, by giving it to Satan. . . .

"See how the temptation was managed; . . . *The tempter came to him.* Note, The Devil is *the tempter,* and therefore he is *Satan—an adversary;* . . . He is an adversary no less watchful than spiteful; . . . When he [Christ our Lord] began to be hungry, and that in a *wilderness,* where there was nothing to be had, then the Devil assaulted him. Note, Want and poverty are a great temptation to discontent and unbelief, and the use of unlawful means for our relief, . . ." (Henry, Vol. V, pages 31–33)

The First Temptation: *"And when the tempter came to him, he said, If thou be the Son of God, command that these stones be made bread."*

Christ's answer: *"But he answered and said, It is written, Man shall not live by bread alone, but by every word that proceedeth out of the mouth of God."* (Matthew 4:3–4)

Henry: "He is himself the eternal Word, and could have produced the mind of God without having recourse to the writings of Moses; but he put honour upon the scripture, and, to set us an example, he appealed to what was written in the law; and he says this to Satan, taking it for granted that he knew well enough what was written. . . . The answer, as all the rest, is taken out of the book of *Deuteronomy,* which signified *the second law,* . . ." (Vol. V, 34)

Ellicott: *"It is written.* —The words of all the three answers to the Tempter come from two chapters of Deuteronomy, one of which (Deuteronomy 6) supplied one of the passages (6:4–9) for the phylacteries or frontlets worn by devout Jews. The fact is every way suggestive. A prominence was thus given to that portion of the book, which made it an essential part of the education of every Israelite. The words which our Lord now uses had, we must believe, been familiar to Him from His childhood, and He had read their meaning rightly.

With them He may have sustained the faith of others in the struggles of the Nazareth home with poverty and want. And now He finds in them a truth which belongs to His high calling as well as to His life of lowliness. 'Not by bread only doth man live, but by the word, *i.e.,* the will, of God.' He can leave His life and all that belongs to it in His Father's hands. In so losing His life, if that should be the issue, He is certain that He shall save it. If His Father has given Him a work to do, He will enable Him to fulfil it. As this act of faith throws us back on the training of the childhood, so we trace its echoes in the after-teaching of the Sermon on the Mount (Matthew 6:25–32), of Matthew 10:39, yet more in that of John 6. The experience of the wilderness clothed the history of the bread from heaven with a new significance. . . ." (*N.T.,* Vol. I, page 15)

The Second Temptation: *"Then the devil taketh him up into the holy city, and setteth him on a pinnacle of the temple, And saith unto him, If you be the Son of God, cast thyself down: for it is written, He shall give his angels charge concerning thee: and in their hands they shall bear thee up, lest at any time thou dash thy foot against a stone."*

Christ's answer: *"Jesus said unto him, It is written again, Thou shalt not tempt the Lord thy God."* (Matthew 4:5–6,7)

Ellicott: *"Taketh him up into the holy city.*—The use of this term to describe Jerusalem (Luke 4:9) is peculiar to St. Matthew among the Evangelists, and is used again by him in 27:53. St. John uses it in Revelation 11:2 of the literal, and in Revelation 21:2 of the heavenly Jerusalem. . . ." (*N.T.,* Vol. I, page 15)

Edersheim comments on this second temptation:

"The Spirit of God had driven Jesus into the wilderness; the spirit of the Devil now carried Him to Jerusalem. Jesus stands on the lofty pinnacle of the Tower, or of the Temple-porch, presumably that on which every day a Priest was stationed to watch, as the pale morning light passed over the hills of Judæa far off to Hebron, to announce it as the signal for offering the morning sacrifice. . . . If we might indulge our imagination, the moment chosen would be just as the Priest had quitted that station. . . . In the Priests' Court below Him the morning-sacrifice has been offered. The massive Temple-gates are slowly opening, and the blasts of the priests' silver trumpets is summoning Israel to begin a new day by appearing before their Lord. Now then let Him descend, Heaven-borne, into the midst of priests and people. What shouts of acclamation would greet His appearance! What homage of worship would be His! The goal can at once be reached, and that at the head of believing Israel . . . The goal might indeed have been reached; but not the Divine goal, nor in God's way—and, as so often, Scripture itself explained and guarded the Divine promise by a preceding Divine command. . . . And thus once more Jesus not only is not overcome, but He overcomes by absolute submission to the Will of God. . . ." (*Messiah, pages 211–12*)

Ellicott: *"It is written again.*—The words are, as already stated, from the chapter that contains one of the passages written on the phylacteries, that were probably used by our Lord Himself. As the words stand in Deuteronomy 6:16, their general meaning is specialised by an historical reference, 'Ye shall not tempt the Lord thy God, as ye tempted Him in Massah.' In the history thus referred to, the sin of the people had been that they questioned the presence of God with them until they saw a supernatural proof of it. They asked, 'Is Jehovah among us, or not?' and that question sprang from unbelief. To have demanded a like proof of His Father's care now would have identified the Son of Man with a like spirit of distrust, and the history of that temptation was therefore a sufficient answer to this. Here, too, a light is thrown on the future teaching of the Christ. The lessons of the wilderness taught Him (the word may seem bold, but it is justified by Hebrew 5:8) to commit Him-

THE TEMPTATION by Gustave Doré

self absolutely to His Father's will. We find almost an echo of what is recorded here in the words which tell us that He forebore to pray for the twelve legions of angels which the Father would have sent him (Matthew 26:53)." (*N.T.,* Vol. I, page 16)

The Third Temptation: *"Again, the devil taketh him up into an exceeding high mountain, and showeth him all the kingdoms of the world, and the glory of them. And saith unto him, All these things will I give thee, if you wilt fall down and worship me."*

Christ's answer: *"Then saith Jesus unto him, Get thee hence, Satan: for it is written, Thou shalt worship the Lord thy God, and him only shalt thou serve."* (Matthew 4:8–9,10)

Henry: ". . . The worst temptation was reserved for the last. . . . What he *showed him—all the kingdoms of the world.* In order to do this, he took him to an *exceeding high mountain*; in hopes of prevailing, as Balak with Balaam, he changed his ground. The pinnacle of the temple is not high enough; the prince of the power of the air must have him further up into his territories. Some think this high mountain was on the other side of Jordan, because there we find Christ next after the temptation, John 1:28–29. Perhaps it was *mount Pisgah,* whence Moses, in communion with God, had all the kingdoms of Canaan shown him. Hither the blessed Jesus was carried for the advantage of a prospect; as if the devil could show him more of the world than he knew already, who made and governed it. . . ." (Vol. V, page 37)

Ellicott: *"All these things will I give thee.*—St. Luke's addition, 'For that is (has been) delivered unto me, and to whomsoever I will I give it,' is full of significance. The offer made by the Tempter rested on the apparent evidence of the world's history. The rulers of the world, its Herods and its Cæsars, seemed to have attained their eminence by trampling the laws of God under foot, and accepting Evil as the Lord and Master of the world. In part, the claim is allowed by our Lord's language and that of his Apostles. Satan is 'the prince of this world' (John 12:31; 14:30). His hosts are 'the world-rulers . . . of darkness' (Ephesians 6:12). In this case the temptation is no longer addressed to the sense of Sonship, but to the love of power. To be a King like other kings, mighty to deliver His people from their oppressors, and achieve the glory which the prophets had predicted for the Christ;—this was possible for Him if only He would go beyond the self-imposed limits of accepting whatsoever His Father ordered for Him.

"*Wilt fall down and worship me.*—The latter word properly expresses, as apparently throughout the New Testament, the homage offered to a king rather than the adoration due to God.

"*Get thee hence, Satan.*—Once more the answer to the Tempter was found in the words of the *Tephillim* and the lessons of childhood. No evidence of power could change the eternal laws of duty. There came to the Son of Man the old command, 'Thou shalt worship the Lord thy God,' as an oracle from heaven, and this, rather than an attempt to refute the claim of sovereignty, was that on which He took His stand. . . . Here, once more, the truth thus affirmed reappears later on. When the chief of the Apostles sought to turn his Master from the appointed path of suffering, he was met, as renewing the same form of temptation which had thus been resisted, with the self-same words. Even Peter had to hear himself rebuked with 'Get thee behind me, Satan' (Matthew 16:23). The use of the formula here, for the first time in the conflict, is significant as implying that in the previous temptations Evil had presented itself in disguise, making sins of distrust appear as acts of faith, while now it showed itself in its naked and absolute antagonism to the divine will." (*N.T.*, Vol. I, pages 16–17)

Henry concludes: ". . . *Then the devil leaveth him. . . .* When the devil left our Saviour, he owned himself fairly beaten; his head was broken by the attempt he made to *bruise Christ's heel.* He left him because he had *nothing in him,* nothing to take hold of; he saw it was to no purpose, and so gave over. Note, The devil though he is an enemy to all the saints, is a conquered enemy. The Captain of our salvation has defeated and disarmed him; we have nothing to do but to *pursue the victory.*

". . . The holy angels came and attended upon our victorious Redeemer; . . . Thus the Son of man did eat angel's food, and, like Elias, is fed by an angel in the wilderness, I Kings 19:4,7. . . .

"Christ was thus succoured after the temptation . . . as our great Melchizdec, who met Abraham when he returned from the battle, and as the angels here ministered to him.

"*Lastly,* Christ, having been thus signalized and made great in the invisible world by the voice of the Father, the descent of the Spirit, his victory over devils, and his dominion over angels, was doubtless qualified to appear in the visible world as the Mediator between God and man; *for consider how great this man was!*" (Henry, Vol. V, pages 38–39)

## BIBLICAL CHILDHOOD OF OUR LORD FULFILLED

"*And when the devil had ended all the temptation, he departed from him for a season. And Jesus returned in the power of the Spirit into Galilee: and there went out a fame of him through all the region round about. And he taught in their synagogues, being glorified of all. And he came to Nazareth, where he had been brought up: and, as his custom was, he went into the synagogue on the sabbath day, and stood up for to read.*" (Luke 4:13–16)

Ellicott states on these passages:

"The narrative that follows, signally interesting in itself, has also the special interest of being peculiar to St. Luke. . . . It is clear that our Lord did not begin His ministry at Nazareth. He came there when His fame was, in some measure, at least, already established.

"*As his custom was.*—This, then, had been His wont before He entered on His work. Children were admitted to the synagogue at the age of five. At thirteen attendance was obligatory. It was open to any man of reputed knowledge and piety, with the sanction of the ruler of the synagogue, to read the lessons (one from the Law and one from the Prophets), and our Lord's previous life had doubtless gained the respect of that officer. Up to this time, it would seem, He had confined Himself to reading. Now He came to preach, after an absence possible of some months, with the new power that had already made Him famous. . . ."

*"And there was delivered unto him the book of the prophet Esaias."* (Luke 4:17)

"The Law—*i.e.*, the Pentateuch—was commonly written on one long roll. The other books, in like manner—singly or combined, according to their length—were written on rolls of parchment, and were unrolled from the cylinder to which they were fastened. Here, it is clear, Isaiah formed a roll by itself. It is a natural inference from the fact that it was given to Him, that it contained the prophetic lesson for the day. In the calendar of modern Jews, the lessons from Isaiah run parallel with those from Deuteronomy. The chapter which He read stands as the second lesson for the day of Atonement. We cannot prove that the existing order obtained in the time of our Lord's ministry, but everything in Judaism rests mainly on old traditions; and there is therefore nothing extravagant in the belief that it was on the day Atonement that the great Atoner thus struck what was the key-note of His whole work."

*"And when he had opened the book, he found the place where it was written, The Spirit of the Lord is upon me. . . ."* (Luke 4:17–18)

"The passage that follows reproduces, with a few important variations, the LXX. version of Isaiah 61:1,2."

". . . *Because he hath anointed me to preach the gospel to the poor; he hath sent me to heal the brokenhearted, to preach deliverance to the captives, and recovering of sight to the blind, to set at liberty them that are bruised, To preach the acceptable year of the Lord. And he closed the book, and he gave it again to the minister, and sat down. And the eyes of all them that were in the synagogue were fastened on him."* (Luke 4:17–20)

JESUS IN THE SYNAGOGUE by J. James Tissot

". . . It is a legitimate inference that the passage which Jesus thus read was one in which He wished men to see the leading idea of His ministry. Glad tidings for the poor, remission of sins, comfort for the mourners, these were what He proclaimed now. These were proclaimed again in the beatitudes of the Sermon on the Mount. We cannot fail to connect the opening words with the descent of the Spirit at His baptism. That was the 'unction from the Holy One' (I John 2:20) which made Him the Christ, the true anointed of the Lord." (Ellicott, *N.T.*, Vol. I, pages 264–65)

Matthew Henry's commentary:

"Those whom God *appoints* to any service he *anoints* for it: 'Because he had sent me, he hath sent his Spirit along with me.' . . .

"Three things he is to preach:—'*Deliverance to the captives.*' The gospel is a proclamation of liberty, like that to Israel in Egypt and in Babylon. By the merit of Christ sinners may be loosed from the bonds of guilt, and by his Spirit and grace from the bondage of corruption. . . .

"*Recovering of sight to the blind.* He came not only by the word of his gospel to bring *light* to them that sat *in the dark*, but by the power of his grace to give sight to them that were *blind*; not only the Gentile world, but every unregenerate soul, that is not only in *bondage*, but in *blindness*, like Samson and Zedekiah. . . .

'*The acceptable year of the Lord.*'. . . It alludes to the year of *release*, or that of *jubilee*, which was an *acceptable year* to servants, who were then set at liberty; to debtors, against whom all actions then dropped; and to those who had mortgaged their lands, for then they returned to them again. Christ came to sound the *jubilee*-trumpet; and blessed were they that heard *the joyful sound*, Psalms 89:15. It was an acceptable time, for it was a day of salvation.

". . . Christ came to be a great *Physician*; for he was sent to *heal the broken-hearted*, to comfort and cure afflicted consciences, to give peace to those that were troubled and humbled for sins, and under a dread of God's wrath against them for them, and to bring them to rest who were weary and heavyladen, under the burden of guilt and corruption.

". . . To be a great *Redeemer.* He not only proclaims liberty to the captives, as Cyrus did to the Jews in Babylon (*Whoever will, may go up*), but he sets at liberty them that are bruised; he doth by his Spirit *incline* and *enable* them to make use of the liberty granted, as then none did but *whose spirit God had stirred up*, Ezra 1:5. He came in God's name to discharge poor sinners that were debtors and prisoners to divine justice. The prophets could but *proclaim liberty*, but Christ, as one having authority, as one that had *power on earth to forgive sins*, came to set at liberty; and therefore this clause is added here. . . .

"Here is Christ's *application* of this text to himself . . . : When he had read it, he *rolled up the book*, and gave it again to the minister, or clerk, that attended, and *sat down* according to the custom of the Jewish

teachers; he *sat daily in the temple, teaching.* (Matthew 26:55). Now he *began* his discourse thus, '*This day is this scripture fulfilled in your ears.* This, which Isaiah wrote by way of prophecy, I have now read to you by way of history.'

"'This day is this scripture fulfilled'." (Henry, Vol. V, page 624)

Ellicott's commentary.

"It is obvious that we have here only the opening words of the sermon preached on the text from Isaiah. There must have been more than this, remembered too vaguely for record, to explain the admiration of which the next clause speaks. But this was what startled them: He had left them as the son of the carpenter—mother, brethren, sisters were still among them—and now He came back claiming to be the Christ, and to make words that had seemed to speak of a far-off glorious dream, as a living and present reality." (*N.T.*, Vol. I, page 265)

The Gospel of Luke: "*And all bare him witness, and wondered at the gracious words which proceeded out of his mouth, And they said, Is not this Joseph's son? And he said unto them, Ye will surely say unto me this proverb, Physician, heal thyself: whatsoever we have heard done in Capernaum, do also here in thy country. And he said, Verily I say unto you, No prophet is accepted in his own country.*" (4:22–24)

Matthew Henry:

". . . Christ's anticipating an objection which he knew to be in the minds of many of his hearers.

"'. . . Because you know that I am the Son of Joseph, your neighbour, you will expect that I should work miracles among you, as I have done in other places; as one would expect that a physician, if he be able, should heal, not only himself, but those of his own family and fraternity, . . . They wanted to have their lame, and blind, and sick, and lepers, healed and helped. . . .'" (Vol. V, page 625)

No wonder a prophet is without honor, and is not

'accepted' in his own country. It was with difficulty that those with whom he had grown up, tried to look beyond their neighbor in Nazareth to the Divine Saviour before them. They had heard of His miracles. They had listened to men from other towns describe the new Spirit in the land. But somehow they could not connect all of this with Jesus of Nazareth, 'the carpenter's son.' As our Lord waited, "with deep longing of soul," as Edersheim puts it, no one in His home town and synagogue was able to discern that Messiah had come. What they dimly perceived was one perhaps who could provide 'loaves and the fishes.'" His friends in Nazareth sought the miracles—like 'magic.' And Jesus had to rebuke this human tendency and turn it to spiritual longings.

*"But I tell you of a truth, many widows were in Israel in the days of Elias, when the heaven was shut up three years and six months, when great famine was throughout all the land; but unto none of them was Elias sent, save unto Sarepta, a city of Sidon, unto a woman that was a widow. And many lepers were in Israel in the time of Eliseus the prophet; and none of them was cleansed, saving Naaman the Syrian."* (Luke 4:25–27)

Matthew Henry: "[Christ gave] pertinent examples of two of the most famous prophets of the Old Testament, who chose to dispense their favours among foreigners rather than among their own countrymen, and that, no doubt by divine direction. . . . Christ himself often met with greater faith among Gentiles than in Israel. And here he mentions both these instances, to show that he did not dispense the favour of his miracles by private respect, but according to God's wise appointment." (Vol. V, page 625–26)

All of Christ's healings were not only by divine appointment but by the external response to our Saviour's internal message of repentance and salvation. Unless there were real spiritual longings to be fulfilled, and a genuine, deep-felt repentance, the miracles would have brought only temporary satisfaction and relief. And because Jesus Christ in Nazareth was only visible as man and not as Messiah, He could not perform any spiritual wonders there.

Edersheim comments on the hearers in the synagogue in Nazareth:

"They had *heard*, and now they would fain have *seen*. But already the holy indignation of Him, Whom they only knew as Joseph's son, was kindled. The turn of matters; their very admiration and expectation; their vulgar, unspiritual comments: it was all so entirely contrary to the Character, the Mission, and the Words of Jesus. . . .

". . . Away He must out of His city; it could not bear His Presence any longer, not even on that holy Sabbath. Out they thrust Him from the Synagogue; forth they pressed Him out of the city; on they followed, and around they beset Him along the road by the brow of the hill on which the city is built—perhaps to that western angle, at present pointed as the site. . . .

IN THE VILLAGES THE SICK WERE BROUGHT UNTO HIM by J. James Tissot

This, with the unspoken intention of crowding Him over the cliff, . . . which there rises abruptly about forty feet out of the valley beneath. . . . If we are correct in indicating the locality, the road here bifurcates, . . . and we can conceive how Jesus, Who hath hitherto, in the silence of sadness, allowed Himself almost mechanically to be pressed onwards by the surrounding crowd, now turned, and by that look of commanding majesty, the forthbreaking of His Divine Being, which ever and ever wrought on those around miracles of subjection, constrained them to halt and give way before Him, while unharmed He passed through their midst. . . . So did Israel of old pass through the cleft waves of the sea, which the wonder-working rod of Moses had converted into a wall of safety. Yet, although He parted from it in judgment, not thus could the Christ have finally and for ever left His own Nazareth. . . ."

Probably resting in Nazareth until the close of the Sabbath, the next day, ". . . Cast out of His own city, Jesus pursued His solitary way towards Capernaum . . . ." (*Messiah,* pages 316–17) This also was a *city of Galilee.* Here He '. . . *taught them on the sabbath days. And they were astonished at his doctrine: for his word was with power.*' (Luke 4:31–32) So Luke concludes this first assault on the Life and Ministry of our Lord—in His own town of Nazareth where He had been brought up.

## THE PROMISE OF LIBERTY TO ISRAEL FULFILLED

As the writer of the first Gospel, Levi-Matthew, the tax-collector, indicated Capernaum, where our Lord passed the first summer of His ministry, was on the sea coast, in the borders of Zabulon and Naphtali. Here again God had Providentially planned the fulfillment of Jesus' prophetic mandate:

*"That it might be fulfilled which was spoken by Isaiah the prophet, saying, The land of Zabulon, and the land of Naphtalim, by the way of the sea, beyond Jordan, Galilee of the Gentiles; The people which sat in darkness saw great light; and to them which sat in the region and shadow of death light is sprung up. From that time Jesus began to preach, and to say, Repent: for the kingdom of heaven is at hand."* (Matthew 4:14–17) It was here in Capernaum that the Lord began to call His first disciples, lowly fishermen, and a tax collector.

*"And as he passed by, he saw Levi the son of Alphæus sitting at the receipt of custom, and said unto him, Follow me. And he arose and followed him."* (Mark 2:14)

Capernaum became the Galilean center for our Lord's preaching in the synagogues of the district. To Matthew, in whose heart the seed had already been planted, so that he was ready and eager to obey Christ's call when it came, that summer was the fulfillment of "the promise of liberty to long-banished Israel." Liberty meant different goals to many at this time, but, we know in view of world history, that what had been started was a revolution, a revolution which would affect the entire world and every individual in it, in every future age.

*"He came unto his own, and his own received him not. But as many as received him, to them gave he power to become the sons of God, even to them that believe on his name: Which are born, not of blood, nor of the will of the flesh, nor of the will of man, but of God. And the Word was made flesh, and dwelt among us, (and we beheld his glory, the glory as of the only begotten of the Father,) full of grace and truth."* (John 1:11–14)

## CHRIST'S LITERARY STYLE

not thought out on the spur of the moment—they were poured out in a living stream when the occasion came—but the water had been gathered into the hidden well for many years before. In the fields and on

The Gospels which record the Life, Ministry, and Teaching of our Saviour, Jesus Christ, represent the crowning glory of the Scriptures. While these writings are all too brief, they contain the Key to Eternal Life,

PHARISEES AND SADDUCEES TEMPT JESUS by J. James Tissot

and reflect all Creation, earth and heaven and man. Their Literary Style is narrative, descriptive, and didactic. And while in translation they represent the highest quality of English expression, they also reflect the individuality of their locale—the Middle East. In order to understand the Literature of the Bible and the Literary Style of our Lord, we must look at where He lived and moved and had His earthly being. It is here we shall discover the influences upon Jesus' literary expression:

James Stalker in his century-old biography, *The Life of Jesus Christ*, writes,

"... Travelers tell us that the spot where He grew up is one of the most beautiful on the face of the earth. Nazareth is situated in a secluded, cup-like valley amid the mountains of Zebulon, just where they dip down into the plain of Esdraelon, with which it is connected by a steep and rocky path. Its white houses, with vines clinging to their walls, are embowered amidst gardens and groves of olive, fig, orange, and pomegranate trees. The fields are divided by hedges of cactus, and enamelled with innumerable flowers of every hue. Behind the village rises a hill five hundred feet in height, from whose summit there is seen one of the most wonderful views in the world—the mountains of Galilee, with snowy Hermon towering above them, to the north; the ridge of Carmel, the coast of Tyre, and the sparkling waters of the Mediterranean, to the west; ... and to the south, the Plain of Esraelon, with the mountains of Ephraim beyond. The preaching of Jesus shows how deeply He had drunk into the essence of natural beauty and revelled in the changing aspects of the seasons. It was when wandering as a lad in these fields that he gathered the images of beauty which He poured out in His parables and addresses. It was on that hill that he acquired the habit of his after-life of retreating to the mountain-tops to spend the night in solitary prayer. The doctrines of His preaching were

113

the mountain-side he had thought them out during the years of happy and undisturbed meditation and prayer." (Stalker, pages 20–21)

In a complementary passage, Alfred Edersheim indicates how *"Nature and Every-day Life"* contributed to His unfolding Mind: "The most superficial perusal of the teaching of Christ must convince how deeply sympathetic He was with nature, and how keenly observant of man. Here there is no contrast between love of the country and the habits of city life; the two are found side by side. On His lonely walks He must have had an eye for the beauty of the lilies of the field, and thought of it, how the birds of the air received their food from an Unseen Hand, and with what maternal affection the hen gathered her chickens under her wing. He had watched the sower or the vinedresser as he went forth to his labour, and read the teaching of the tares which sprang up among the wheat. To Him the vocation of the shepherd must have been full of meaning, as he led, and fed, and watched his flock, spoke to his sheep with well-known voice, brought them to the fold, or followed, and tenderly carried back, those that had strayed, ever ready to defend them, even at the cost of his own life. Nay, He even seems to have watched the habits of the fox in its secret lair. But he also equally knew the joys, the sorrows, the wants and sufferings of the busy multitude. The play in the market, the marriage processions, the funeral rites, the wrongs of injustice and oppression, the urgent harshness of the creditor, the bonds and prison of the debtor, the palaces and luxury of princes and courtiers, the self-indulgence of the rich, the avarice of the covetous, the exactions of the tax-gatherer, and the oppression of the widow by unjust judges, had all made an indelible impression on His mind. . . ." (Edersheim, *Messiah*, page 175)

Stalker speaks of the form of Jesus' preaching, a form which became our written heritage in the Gospels:

". . . The Oriental mind does not work in the same way as the mind of the West. Our thinking and speak-ing, when at their best, are fluent, expansive, closely reasoned. The kind of discourse which we admire is one which takes up an important subject, divides it out into different branches, treats it fully under each of the heads, closely articulates part to part, and closes with a moving appeal to the feelings, so as to sway the will to some practical result. The Oriental mind, on the contrary, loves to brood long on a single point, to turn it round and round, to gather up all the truth about it in a focus, and pour forth in a few pointed and memorable words. It is concise, epigrammatic, oracular. A Western speaker's discourse is a systematic structure, or like a chain in which link is firmly knit to link; an Oriental's is like the sky at night, full of innumerable burning points shining forth from a dark background.

". . . Such was the form of the teaching of Jesus. It consisted of numerous sayings, everyone of which contained the greatest possible amount of truth in the smallest possible compass, and was expressed in language so concise and pointed as to stick in the memory like an arrow. . . .

". . . But there was another characteristic of the form of Jesus' teaching. It was full of figures of speech. He thought in images. He had ever been a loving and accurate observer of nature around Him—of the colors of the flowers, the ways of the birds, the growth of the trees, the vicissitudes of the seasons—and an equally keen observer of the ways of men in all parts of life—in religion, in business, in the home. The result was that He could neither think nor speak without His thought running into the mould of some natural image. His preaching was alive with such references, and therefore full of color, movement and changing forms. There were no abstract statements in it; they were all changed into pictures. Thus, in His sayings, we can still see the aspects of the country and the life of the time as in a panorama—the lilies, whose gorgeous beauty His eyes feasted on, waving in the fields; the sheep following the shepherd; the broad and narrow city gates; the virgins with their lamps awaiting in the darkness the bridal procession; the Pharisee with his broad phylacteries and the publican with bent head at prayer together in the temple; the rich man seated in his palace at a feast, and the beggar lying at his gate with the dogs licking his sores; and a hundred other pictures that lay bare the inner and minute life of the time, over which history in general sweeps heedlessly with majestic stride. (Stalker, pages 65–67)

## JESUS' USE OF THE PARABLE

"But the most characteristic form of speech He made use of was the parable. It was a combination of the two qualities already mentioned—concise, memorable expression, and a figurative style. It used an incident, taken from common life and rounded into a gem-like picture, to set forth some corresponding truth in the higher and spiritual region. It was a favorite Jewish mode of putting truth, but Jesus imparted to it by far the richest and most perfect development. About one-third of all His sayings which have been preserved to us consists of parables. This shows how they stuck in the memory. . . . The Prodigal Son, the Sower, the Ten Virgins, the Good Samaritan,—these and many others are pictures hung up in millions of minds. What passages in the greatest masters of expression—in Homer, in Virgil, in Dante, in Shakespeare—have secured for themselves so universal a hold on men, or been felt to be so fadelessly fresh and true? . . . Jesus took the commonest objects and incidents around Him —the sewing of a piece of cloth on an old garment, the bursting of an old bottle, the children playing in the marketplace at weddings and funerals, or the tumbling of a hut in a storm—to change them into perfect pictures, and to make them the vehicles for conveying to the world immortal truth. No wonder the crowds followed Him! Even the simplest could delight in such pictures and carry away as a life-long possession the expression at least of His ideas, though it might require the thought of centuries to pierce their crystalline depths. There never was speaking so simple yet so profound, so pictorial yet so absolutely true.

"Such were the qualities of His Style. . . ." (Stalker, pages 65–68)

In his study of *The Literature of the Bible*, Leland Ryken makes the following evaluation of Jesus' use of

PARABLE OF THE GOOD SAMARITAN

the parable in his speaking and teaching:

"The parable was one of the commonest forms used by Jesus—so common, in fact, that Mark comments that Jesus 'did not speak to them without a parable' (Mark 4:34). It is evident that Jesus did not share the bias against fiction that has existed in Western thought. We might profitably ask why Jesus used fiction as His medium.

"Makers of literature, including Jesus, use fiction partly because it appeals to a deep-seated human capacity to enjoy an imaginative story. Like the other human faculties, the imagination asks to be exercised. By using fictional stories, an author satisfied this unconscious as well as conscious capacity for imaginative narrative.

"A second function served by fiction is that it is often the best or even the only medium by which a writer can express his vision. Makers of fiction have something true to say about life, but they can say it only by embodying it in an imaginative projection of life. The imagined world of fiction, rather than the real world of fact, is sometimes the world where the issues can be seen in greatest clarity. It is evident that Jesus often looked upon fiction as the most accurate form for expressing His teachings." (Ryken, page 314)

Even as the Literature of our Lord was first of all an Oral Literature—spoken from the lips of our Saviour—His delivery or His Speaking Style was a basic part of the message. Even as later we would read these Teachings rather than hear them, there was a characteristic quality which individualized both spoken and written word. Stalker identifies these qualities as—

". . . Authority: The people were astonished at His doctrine, for he taught them as one having authority, and not as the scribes.' . . .

". . . Boldness: 'Lo, He speaketh boldly.' . . .

". . . Power: 'His word was with power.' . . ." And lastly: "A fourth quality which was observed in His preaching, and was surely a very prominent one, was Graciousness: 'They wondered at the gracious words which proceeded out of His mouth.' In spite of His tone of authority and His fearless and scathing attacks on the times, there was diffused over all He said a glow of grace and love. Here especially His character spoke. How could He who was the incarnation of love help letting the glow and warmth of the heavenly fire that dwelt in Him spread over His words? The scribes of the time were hard, proud, and loveless. They flattered the rich and honored the learned, but of the great mass of their hearers they said, 'This people, which knoweth not the law, is cursed.' But to Jesus every soul was infinitely precious. It mattered not under what humble dress or social deformity the pearl was hidden; it mattered not even beneath what rubbish and filth of sin it was buried; He never missed it for a moment. Therefore, He spoke to His hearers of every grade with the same respect. Surely it was the divine love itself, uttering itself from the innermost recess of the divine being, that spoke in the parables of the fifteenth of Luke . . . ." (Stalker, pages 68–69,71)

Jesus Christ transformed Literature just as He transformed every field of human endeavor. Jesus presented to the world a new idea of man, the Christian Idea of man, which considered each individual as of infinite value and worth, equally created by God. Unlike any

PARABLE OF THE PRODIGAL SON by Gustave Doré

other type of literature ever expressed, closest to the Literature of the Old Testament, and yet unique, Jesus addressed the internal heart and character of the individual. In images of daily life which He had pondered since childhood, He spoke of the primary concerns of life. His first great teaching, the Sermon on the Mount, contains numerous examples of His Literary Style and expression. Beginning with the Beatitudes Jesus set forth the character of blessedness in what Matthew Henry denotes as "the agenda of Christianity, the things to be done." Here is our Lord's contrast to the character of rabbinism, the blessings of a godly life, lived in opposition to the world's concept of a heroic character, one devoted to the true blessings of liberty by obedience to God's spiritual law.

# LET OUR YOUTH
# BE INSTRUCTED

by Rosalie J. Slater

# THE CHRISTIAN
# IDEA OF THE CHILD

by Carole G. Adams

"I Love to Hear the Story" from *The Children's Book of Hymns*
Illustrated by Cicely Mary Barker, 1929

# LET OUR YOUTH
# BE INSTRUCTED

## THE BIBLE AS A CLASSIC

This section considers the Biblical Foundations of Literature, presenting both the internal and external functions of a Biblical education. This Biblical education begins in the family and with a Biblical childhood—a preparation for serving Christ and country. Secondly, a Biblical education can be a foundation for the study of the "Literature and Character of Liberty."

We have discussed briefly some of the implications of a family education and its contributions to producing a Biblical home-life and childhood. Our documentation has been the Bible itself, a record which was important to the Founders of the American Christian Republic.

Let us now consider the study of the Bible as Literature. Let us learn to accept it as a classic, if not *the classic* in world literature. To begin with, what did our pastors in America think of the Bible as Literature?

When young Timothy Dwight, grandson of Jonathan Edwards, gave the Commencement Address at Yale in 1772, a college of which he would someday be president, he chose for his topic the following: *A Dissertation on the History, Eloquence, and Poetry of the Bible.* (See *Consider & Ponder,* pages 224–230.)

From his background of Biblical and classical literature, Dwight could speak authoritatively on his theme that the Bible surpassed all other literature. By comparison to the finest secular authors, the authors of the divine Book far exceeded in literary excellence all others. As Timothy Dwight developed his subject he made these comparisons:

The Bible contains poetry more sublime than Homer, more correct and tender than Virgil;

. . . . contains eloquence greater than Cicero and Demosthenes;

. . . . contains history more majestic and spirited than Livy and Robertson;

. . . . on every page the boldest metaphors, the most complete images, the liveliest descriptions;

. . . . a divine morality unsurpassed by Plato.

Timothy Dwight spoke from a knowledge of literature which he, like a majority of our founding pastors, future statesmen, and a large segment of the colonists, had mastered in their education. He knew the Bible as Literature because he had studied much of the world's great literature.

One hundred years ago a pastor might still be well educated in the Bible as Literature, and could compare it to world classics. In 1866, Pastor LeRoy J. Halsey wrote in the introductory pages of his book *The Literary Attractions of the Bible; or A Plea for the Word of God, Considered as a Classic*:

"It is greatly to be desired that our children and youth should grow up with the conviction firmly fixed in their minds, that the Bible is a classic of the very highest authority in all matters of education, taste, and genius; that it holds the same place of preeminence in the republic of letters which it holds in the Church of God. . . .

"We must not let them forget, that it is, at once, the most ancient, the most sublime, the most wonderful of all the classics. We do not discard Homer and Virgil from the classics because they contain a religion, even an absurd, fabulous religion; why, then, should we underrate, or disparage the classical claims of the Bible, because it contains a religion, and that, the only true religion? . . . " (Halsey, pages 18–19)

Pastor Halsey was addressing his remarks chiefly to the public schools of his day, for they, like the Christian schools, were still teaching a curriculum largely based upon a total acceptance of the Word of God as foundational to education.

Pastor Halsey also knew what few of our pastors in American preach today, namely the connection of the Bible to our basic American institutions:

" . . . As a book of religion, around which cluster all our hopes of immortality, the Bible has merits of the very highest order; . . . But, aside from the religion which it reveals to us, and the good news of salvation which it brings us, the Bible has other attractions.

"It is the book of our learning, not less than our religion; the basis of our civilization, not less than our salvation. It is the charter of our rights and liberties, as truly as it is the oracle of our faith, the manual of our devotions, and the anchor of our hopes. It has moulded into shape, and it has quickened into life, the whole body of our secular learning, as well as our theology.

"It has breathed its own vital spirit into all our science, literature, legislation, philosophy, social and political institutions. It has led the van of ancient and of modern civilization in its march around the globe." (Halsey, pages 13–14)

To form a character for liberty we need to know the literature of liberty and that history and literature begin in the Bible. What better step can we take in the restoration of our American Christian Constitutional Republic than to restore the study of the Bible as Literature? The more we learn of the Bible's literary excellence the better we will be able to draw a comparison with the world's finest literature. Just as Pastor Timothy Dwight knew the literary excellence of the Bible because he could compare it with his own study of all literature, so should we in our generation restore our own knowledge of these fields of study. And we can begin with the Bible, adding what we can of the ancient classical writers.

## A BIBLE OF LITERARY EXCELLENCE

To study the Bible as Literature is to study the 1611 King James version—a translation done by forty-seven scholars, men who not only worked with the English language at it finest flowering, but who had the advantage of the earliest English versions done by Wyclif, Tindale, and Matthew Coverdale.

"The supreme literary excellence of the Authorized Version has made it the greatest of English classics. Owing to the superb beauty of its language, the Bible has an importance in our literature which is unparalleled elsewhere. . . .

"It is almost impossible to exaggerate the influence of that Version on the English language and English thought. The Bible made English Puritanism; and the Puritan tradition has fostered in the British and American peoples most of their best and distinctive qualities. From the Bible Milton and Bunyan took the inspiration of their poetry and allegory. In the Bible

Cromwell and the Pilgrim Fathers found that which made them honourable, self-reliant, and stedfast. Bible in hand, Wesley and Whitefield transformed their country. . . ." (Drinkwater, Vol. I, page 74)

## BEGIN YOUR LITERARY STUDY OF THE BIBLE

In *The Noah Plan Literature Curriculum Guide*, examine Chapter Two, "Learning the Literature of the Bible" as the "Source and Seedbed of Literature and Liberty," and look at the chart for Researching the Literary Elements of the Bible.

How might you begin to develop your Literary Study of the Bible beginning first with "The Language, Style and Expression of the Bible?" Let us RESEARCH 'language.'

On the first page of his "Introduction" to the 1828 *An American Dictionary of the English Language*, Noah Webster in his definition of 'language' makes two important points: ". . . [L]anguage belongs exclusively to intellectual and intelligent beings, and among terrestrial beings, to man only; for no animal on earth, except man, can pronounce words." Webster then goes on to discuss animal sounds in contrast to language as a means of communicating thoughts or ideas. In his discussion of the "Origin of Language," Noah Webster makes the statement, ". . . Hence we may infer that language was bestowed on Adam in the same manner as all his other faculties and knowledge, by supernatural power; or in other words, was of divine origin. . . . It is therefore probable that *language* as well as the faculty of speech, was the *immediate gift of God*. . . ."

Let us REASON. What kind of language do we find in the Bible? In what ways does language in the Bible differ from the language we find in other books? Why? In Genesis, Chapter One, find those words which define GOD. Look up the definition for 'God' in Webster. The word 'God' and the word 'good' in the Anglo Saxon are written the same. What can we infer about 'God' and 'goodness' from the Language, Style, and Expression of the words which describe this foundational chapter in the Bible? Does the Language, Style, and Expression of the King James Version complement the Creator?

Let us RELATE our study of language in Genesis One and consider the word 'Let.' How is this word used in connection with 'God' and how might it be classified governmentally in the lives of students? Why is this a marvellous word to reflect upon?

Lastly, let us RECORD the results of our study of the Language, Style, and Expression of the Bible from the first chapter of Genesis. How will you record the distinctives of the literary expression of the ideas, thoughts and feelings which God's Word brings forth?

Our children study God's Word. Let us help them understand its beauty of style, choice of words, power of expression. The King James translation was especially addressed to the cultivation of the reflective individual—the man or woman or child of God's creating. Words reflect depths of meaning and the words chosen by the 1611 translators of the Bible allow the individual to meditate and grow in the understanding of the spiritual ideas which are the seeds sown in rich language. Levels of understanding can begin with the youngest child and deepen with internal growth.

David wrote in PSALM 19:1–4

The heavens declare the glory of God;
    and the firmament sheweth his handywork.
Day unto day uttereth speech,
    and night unto night sheweth knowledge.

There is no speech nor language
    where their voice is not heard.
Their line is gone out through all the earth,
    and their words to the end of the world. . . .

And in PSALM 143:5, David stated,

I remember the days of old;
    I meditate on all thy works;
    I muse on the work of thy hands.

Perhaps these reflections on God's glorious creation first came to the shepherd boy, David, as he lay on his back in the pastures with his sheep during starry nights, secure in the strength of the Lord.

Oh, that our children might find Him through the glorious Language, Style, and Expression of His Word!

## REVIEW THE LITERARY ELEMENTS OF THIS SECTION

The revival of home education in America comes at a most Providential moment in our history. There is no single element in American life which contributes more significantly to the success of Christian Constitutional government than the Christian home in our Republic. It is in the home where the foundations of character are laid. It is in the home where 'the art of self-government' is learned and practiced because it can be exemplified by Fathers and Mothers. With home education now accepting its responsibility for the Biblical education of children in America, we have an opportunity to take back our responsibility for maintaining those blessings of Liberty which God has bestowed upon us as a unique nation in the History of Liberty. And if the homes in America are willing to begin the restoration of the Biblical foundations of literature we will again see a real return to that quality of academics which once characterized this land just before we began to produce our important writings on Liberty.

The Biblical homelife and the Biblical childhood of Moses, Samuel, David, John the Baptist, and our Lord Jesus Christ, which we have considered here, enabled those individuals to fulfill their God-appointed ministries in the History of Liberty. They also provide us with a record of the Character for Liberty. We may ask, "How can American Christians, living in a different period of time, and in a distinct Land of Liberty, prepare our homes so that we too can provide our children with a Biblical childhood?" With this question uppermost in our hearts and minds, we seek, with the Lord's direction, to restore American's Christian History and government. As we have learned from the brief studies in this section, the foundation of Liberty is found in the Word of God, and the Literature of Liberty has its first expression there. If we are dedicated to restoring the character of Liberty in ourselves, in our children, and, ultimately in our nation, we must begin with the Bible. How do we begin to make a study of the History and Character of Liberty from the Literature of the Bible?

*The Noah Plan Literature Curriculum Guide* Chapter Two (pp. 69–82) deals with "Learning the Literature of the Bible." In the following chart we have taken the individuals referred to in this section of our book and summarized them under the "Literary Elements of the Bible." If you now will follow these references in your own Bible you can make your own expanded chart as a preparation for presenting a beginning lesson for your family or students.

Just as Hannah More found her appreciation of the Providential deliverance of Moses enhanced by writing a Sacred Drama, *Moses in the Bulrushes,* so your children will be able to reflect upon this true story from the standpoint of its literary excellence as one of the most dramatic and far reaching events in the History of Liberty. While Mrs. More's eighteenth century language slows us down a bit, yet, it will enable us to fully savour the emotions and feelings of all concerned in these Biblical events.

Of course, you will be led with your children to ponder the two educations of Moses and to imagine just what this remarkable family taught their Providentially delivered brother. Aaron and Miriam, who were to play critical roles in Moses' future ministry, must have spent many hours with their parents Jochebed and Amram teaching Moses about his Founding Fathers—Abraham, Isaac, Jacob, and Joseph—those Patriarchs recorded in Genesis. Here, Moses would learn about the unique character of a people whose history he would one day record. And how he must have pondered the years that Joseph spent in Egypt when that nation worshipped only one God.

And despite the longer hours, days, months and years that Moses would have to spend at the court of Pharaoh in the Palace with his adopted mother, Thermutis, Princess of Egypt, yet consider which education was to have the greatest influence upon his life. What he learned of the One God of Israel was able to outshine the mysticism of the religion of Egypt with her multitude of gods and priests. Pagan life and education were unable to dislodge Moses' true vision of liberty, dignity, and character. He did not confuse his God-given individuality and identity despite the fact that it would be many long years before he would be ready to speak to God "face to face."

## EGYPT IN THE HISTORY OF LIBERTY

The Principle Approach to any subject is its relationship to the History, Literature, and character of Liberty. The 4 R's of researching, reasoning, relating and recording become very useful as we begin a historical and literary study of the Bible.

If we are to properly understand the miraculous events in the life of Moses and in the History of Israel, we need to place Egypt as one of God's instruments in that history. As Dr. Alfred Edersheim states in his article at the beginning of Exodus in his *Bible History*:

". . . [W]hat Greece was to the world at the time of Christ, that and much more had Egypt been when the children of Israel became a God-chosen nation. Not that in either case the truth of God needed help from the wisdom of this world. On the contrary, in one sense, it stood opposed to it. And yet while history pursued seemingly its independent course, and philosophy, science, and the arts advanced apparently without any reference to Revelation, all were in the end made subservient to the furtherance of the kingdom of God. And so it always is. God marvellously uses natural means for supernatural ends, and maketh all things work together to His glory as well as for the good of His people."

One important reason, it seems that God placed the history of Israel in Egypt and the history of Christ in Rome, was to put these major stepping stones in the History of Liberty in full view of the known world. ". . . When standing before King Agrippa, St. Paul could confidently appeal to the publicity of the history of Christ, as enacted not in some obscure corner of a barbarous land, but in full view of the Roman world: 'For this thing was not done in a corner.' Acts 26:26. And so Israel's bondage also and God's marvellous deliverance took place on no less conspicuous a scene than that of the ancient world-empire of Egypt." (Edersheim, *O.T.*, Vol. II, pages 9–10)

What might be some first steps in becoming better acquainted with the Egypt of Moses' time?

# Learning the Literature of the Bible

*Source and Seedbed of Literature and Liberty*

## Researching the Literary Elements of the Bible

| Subject | Settings | Characterizations | Plot Elements | Themes | Style/Writings |
|---|---|---|---|---|---|
| Moses | Hebrew home and Palace in Egypt<br><br>The "backside of the desert"<br><br>At Sinai and in the Wilderness | Egypt: 40 years home and palace<br><br>Desert: 40 years God's preparation of Moses<br><br>Wilderness: 40 years service to God and nation Israel | Life Providentially spared<br><br>Instructed by God to deliver Israel from bondage<br><br>Talked to God "face to face"<br><br>Instrument of God's Law to Israel | Providential<br><br>Preparation<br><br>Deliverance<br><br>Teacher of God's Law | The Pentateuch<br><br>The Song of Moses<br><br>Historian and Instructor in government of the individual and nation |
| Samuel | Home of Elkanah and Hannah<br><br>The Temple Israel | The Child Prophet<br><br>The Character of a Prophet, Priest, and Judge | Providential birth<br><br>Temple ministry under Eli<br><br>Work of Revival in Israel<br><br>Founding the Schools of the Prophets<br><br>Monarchy established | Holiness in God's Temple<br><br>A people to love the Lord<br><br>The Council of Prophets<br><br>The Character of Kings | His recorded words in First and Second Samuel |
| David | Birthplace in Bethlehem<br><br>Hillsides of Judea<br><br>In flight in the wilderness<br><br>King in Hebron | Shepherd, Play of the Harp<br><br>Military Man<br><br>Friend<br><br>King<br><br>Man after God's Heart | Relationship to first King, Saul<br><br>Friend of Prince Jonathan<br><br>Three times anointed to serve God<br><br>A proto-type of Christ | The character of a ruler, "must rule in the fear of the Lord"<br><br>Fallibility of man | The Psalms of David<br><br>His recorded words in First and Second Samuel, First and Second Kings, and First Chronicles |
| John the Baptist | Home: "hill country of Judea"<br><br>Preaching: deserts of Judea, countryside about Jordan<br><br>Death: Machaerus Castle, Dead Sea | Old Testament Prophet in New Testament era<br><br>The Forerunner of the Saviour | 400 years of prophetic silence<br><br>Linked Old and New Testaments<br><br>A Witness to the Truth<br><br>Martyred by Herod | Revival and Repentance.<br><br>The "voice crying in the Wilderness" announcing the coming of the "Lamb of God which taketh away the sin of the world" | Prophetic words of Isaiah fulfilled<br><br>Words recorded in the four Gospels |

# Learning the Literature of the Bible

*Source and Seedbed of Literature and Liberty*

## Researching the Literary Elements of the Bible

| Subject | Settings | Characterizations | Plot Elements | Themes | Style/Writings |
|---|---|---|---|---|---|
| Jesus | Home in Nazareth | The God-man | Biblical Childhood | The Life of Blessedness | His Gospel words reflect the Old Testament teachings of Moses and the Prophets concerning Him |
| | Galilean | *Names for Jesus Christ in Scripture:* | Education in the Scriptures | The Message of Repentance and Salvation | |
| | Synagogue | Alpha and Omega | Appearances at the Temple | The Lamb of God offered as a sacrifice for sin | |
| | The Temple at Jerusalem | Ancient of Days | On the banks of the Jordan | | |
| | On the banks of the Jordan | Anointed of the Lord | In the wilderness with "wild beasts" | | |
| | In the wilderness with wild beasts | Beloved of God | Preaching, teaching, healing, redeeming, in Palestine | | |
| | Palestine | Branch of Righteousness | Arrest and trials | | |
| | Jerusalem: Sanhedrin | Bread of Life | Crucifixion | | |
| | Antonia Fortress | Bridegroom | Resurrection | | |
| | Golgotha | Bright and Morning Star | Ascension | | |
| | | Captain of Salvation | | | |
| | | Carpenter's son | | | |
| | | Chief cornerstone | | | |
| | | Day star | | | |
| | | Dayspring | | | |
| | | Door of the Sheep | | | |
| | | Emmanuel | | | |
| | | First Fruits | | | |
| | | Holy One of God | | | |
| | | I Am | | | |
| | | Jesus of Nazareth | | | |
| | | Lamb of God | | | |
| | | Lily of the valleys | | | |
| | | Lion of the tribe of Judah | | | |
| | | Living Bread | | | |
| | | Rock | | | |
| | | Sun of Righteousness | | | |
| | | True Vine, etc. | | | |

RESEARCHING:

Find some books and maps on the subject of Egypt in Bible times. Actually, the subject of Egypt will recur a number of times in Ancient and Modern history, so your efforts to deepen your knowledge of the history, geography, literature of the Bible will be helpful to your total educational program. Your public library may have some treasures that have not recently been checked out. Your Bible Book store may be a source of help especially on maps of Bible lands. Here are some titles we have found helpful:

*Lands of the Bible* by Samuel Terrien, Simon and Schuster, New York, 1957. This is a 96-page book, 10" x 13" with colorful maps and illustrations. It is from the Golden Book series of simplified books.

*Everyday Life in Bible Times*, National Geographic Society, Washington, D.C., 1966. This 448-page book has many maps, illustrations, and charts which provide a picture of the daily life of Bible times as well as its history. As an introduction to deeper study it may suggest special areas of interest for research.

Watch also for *The Noah Plan Bible Curriculum Guide* by Rosalie J. Slater, which is under production.

REASONING:

With maps you and your students can reason out where Moses lived, where he spent some forty years in the desert, and the route of the Exodus. Think about Egypt and this portion of the world and refer to Arnold Guyot in both *Christian History* and *Teaching and Learning*, and consider why he classified Africa as a continent of nature. What kinds of implications does this have for Egypt in world history and especially as we study it in Biblical literature?

RELATING:

Read in the Bible the Providential events in Moses' life and especially consider how these events were to shape and form the nation Israel. What effect did Moses' experiences with God have upon our nation America? Would America be the same without Moses?

RECORDING:

A special notebook for Learning the Literature of the Bible will help you keep a record of what means the most to you and your family in these beginning lessons.

Lastly, compare the Style and Writings of each of the five individuals we have introduced in this book: Moses, Samuel, David, John the Baptist, and our Lord Jesus Christ. How does an historian write—and sing? How does a prophet speak to other men when God has spoken to him? Can you record the events in David's life which provoked the writing of some of his psalms? And does John the Baptist sound different from Old Testament prophets—compare the differences and the similarities. Finally, can you find those passages in the Gospels which represent statements which characterize our Lord's many-faceted infinite character? What makes him sound at one time like the "Lion of the Tribe of Judah" and another time like "The Rose of Sharon?" See how many of His *names* you can trace from the Old Testament into the New Testament. What a blessed research project!

The Leading and Teaching of the Holy Spirit is so precious to an individual Christian that we always hesitate to make too many suggestions for fear of depriving you of the Holy Teaching and Learning.

Once you have gone a short distance into the study of the Bible as Literature, you will find yourselves drawn to the Word more than ever, for here is the History and Character of Liberty which has inspired men in all centuries and of all nations. It was an especial inspiration to the Founding Fathers and Mothers of the American Christian Republic.

# THE CONTRIBUTION OF
# BIBLE SCHOLARS
# TO BIBLICAL CHILDHOOD

## by Rosalie J. Slater

Our knowledge of the Bible deepens our lives. America's heritage from England includes, not only the Bible translations, but also the contribution of Biblical scholarship from many individuals. What could be more inspiring than research into Bible, especially when scholars of Hebrew background become converted and add much to our knowledge of both the Old Testament and the New.

### ALFRED EDERSHEIM

For "Biblical Childhood" we are particularly blessed with the availability of the works of Alfred Edersheim (1825–1889). From Dr. Edersheim's *The Life and Times of Jesus the Messiah*, we can learn of the land of Galilee where "... Jesus spent by far the longest part of His life upon earth.... A more beautiful country—hill, dale, and lake—could scarcely be imagined...." Dr. Edersheim calls it "... the smiling landscape...." It was the home of "... generous spirits, of warm impulsive hearts, of intense nationalism, of simple manners, and of earnest piety." Edersheim contrasts the land of Galilee with Judea "... which at that time was comparatively desolate, barren, gray...." But here was developed the critical Rabbinism which had "contempt for all that was Galilean...." This helps us understand why the people saw in Jesus a new spirit rather than the legalism of the Scribes and Pharisees.

Under the subheading of "Christ's Sympathy with Nature and Man," we learn of "... the religious influences in the family, so blessedly different from that of neglect, exposure, and even murder of children among the heathen, or their education by slaves; ..." "The love of parents to children, ... the reverence towards parents, as a duty higher than any of outward observance; and the love of brethren, which Jesus learned in His home, form so to speak, the natural basis of many of the teachings of Jesus...." (Edersheim, *Messiah*, pages 155–57, 174–75)

I encourage readers to purchase Edersheim's *The Life and Times of Jesus the Messiah*, complete in one volume, Hendrickson Publishers, ISBN 0-943575-83-4. Also available is his *Sketches of Jewish Social Life*, from Hendrickson: hardcover ISBN 1-56563-138-2 and paperback ISBN 1-56563-005-X. The blessing of this 307-page volume, shorter than the mammoth *Jesus the Messiah*, is that it "... transport[s] the reader into the land of Palestine at the time of our Lord and of His apostles, ..." (page vii) Of particular interest to the readers of *The Family and the Nation: Biblical Childhood*, are those chapters dealing with "Jewish Homes," "The

Upbringing of Jewish Children," "Subjects of Study," "Home Education in Israel," and others, plus there are two appendices, an index, and a six-page Index to Scripture References.

## CHARLES JOHN ELLICOTT, D.D.

Ellicott, Lord Bishop of Gloucester and Bristol, has introduced English readers to an Old Testament and New Testament Commentary, represented by various writers. These volumes published in London in 1884, were researched by Miss Verna Hall as she unfolded her volumes in *The Christian History of the Constitution of the United States of America*, Vol. I: *Christian Self-Government* and Vol. II: *Christian Self-Government with Union*, and *The Christian History of the American Revolution: Consider and Ponder*.

The F.A.C.E. Research Library includes these volumes with Miss Hall's pencil marks. Noteworthy are Ellicott's references to the fact "that the narrative of Holy Scripture is the record of the providential government of the world rather than of the events and issues of merely human history. (Ellicott, *O.T.*, Vol. I, "Preface," page IX) Ellicott also reaffirms "that the Old Testament is the record of the long preparation of mankind for that which every true heart in every age had dimly longed for—redemption of salvation through Jesus Christ." (*O.T.*, Vol. I, "Preface," page XI)

One of the most remarkable contributions which Miss Hall brought to us was the recording of the most significant English translation of Holy Scripture. In the New Testament Commentary Preface, she particularly marks the work of Wycliffe, William Tyndale, and Coverdale to whom we owe "the first complete translation of the whole Bible published in 1535." (*O.T.*, Vol. I, "Preface," page XXII) Miss Hall particularly notes the contribution of the Geneva Bible which was printed at Geneva, with an introductory epistle by Calvin. "It was also the first translation printed in Roman type and so presenting a clearer and easier page for the reader. . . . Of all English versions before that of 1611, it was by far the most popular. Size, price, type, notes, division into verses, made it for more than half-a-cen-

tury the household Bible of the English people . . . . It was the Geneva version that gave birth to the great Puritan party, and sustained it through its long conflict in the reigns of Elizabeth and James." (*O.T.*, Vol. I, "Preface," page XXIV) The Pilgrims brought the Geneva Bible to America as did the settlers of Jamestown.

## ARTHUR W. PINK

Arthur Pink was born in England, but died in Scotland in 1952. He had a widespread ministry which included Australia and the United States. With a Puritan and Reformed position his studies of the Scriptures brought Biblical principles and Biblical leaders close to our twentieth century students. Beginning with *Gleanings in Genesis, Gleanings in Exodus, Gleanings in Joshua, Gleanings from Elisha, Life of David*, and *Gleanings from Paul*, we have a detailed presentation of God's Word made applicable to our times. "The work of God the Father and God the Holy Spirit receive their proper emphasis as well as the work of the Son." Once again these volumes in our Biblical library carry the many pencil marks of Verna Hall as she related God's Word to the history of American government and education.

As we contemplate the education of our children it is worthy to note how God prepared His leaders, Pink comments on the forty years Moses spent in "the backside of the desert," and he indicates: " 'The backside of the desert' is where men and things, the world and self, present circumstances and their influences, are all valued at what they are really worth. . . . The heart that has found itself in the presence of God at 'the backside of the desert' has right thoughts about everything." (*Biblical Childhood*, page 24)

## MATTHEW HENRY

Henry was called the 'Prince of Bible Commentators.' Through many years Miss Hall and I studied his commentaries daily. We wore out several complete sets. On our automobile travels we carried the six volumes with us and sometimes read portions together.

Matthew Henry was the son of Rev. Philip Henry who preached in England during a difficult time. He was often restrained from his ministry and his home cleared out if several persons were found with him. He expected his children to pay good attention to all their good preaching and checked what they learned from each sermon. He sent Matthew to study the law, but his son was too deeply drawn by the Scripture and became a minister and writer of the Word of God. His commentaries have drawn millions into a closer walk with God, and a deeper understanding of His Word and its relationship to their lives.

## G. CAMPBELL MORGAN

We acknowledge another great English Bible Scholar who spent many years in America and was the author of more than fifty books. G. Campbell Morgan, in *The Unfolding Message of the Bible: The Harmony and Unity of the Scriptures*, stated:

"Take the Psalms, or the Prophets: they are all set against a background of history. . . . But that is only one element. The other is this. It is a record of divine government from the beginning to the end. . . . Human history and divine government. . . . This is a library, but it is a great continuous history of humanity, and the account of divine government, and at the center of everything is Christ and His Cross."

The most important knowledge which we can have and give our children is a love of the Scriptures and a continuous study of them.

## THE DICKSON BIBLE—A BIBLE TO TEACH IN BOTH HOME AND SCHOOL

The life of a Christian is wrapped up in the Bible. It is the most important library of books ever assembled. It is the most providential book in the world because its purpose is to record the amazing series of events which brought forth the Saviour of mankind. There is an internal aspect of the Bible which is often neglected. Here is an example:

One of the most powerful events in the Book of Genesis begins in Chapter 37. It is the history of Joseph, beloved son of Jacob, and his brethren. Jealousy of Joseph caused his brothers to sell him into slavery in Egypt. But God had a special role for Joseph to play in the history of Israel and in the bringing forth of the Messiah. The Dickson Bible in a special section of Outstanding Facts, reveals "Joseph's Place in Israel's History." Joseph's ability to interpret dreams placed him in the Egyptian Empire next to Pharaoh. He averted the famine of that region, and his forgiveness of his brethren brought God's chosen people into Egypt to preserve them. We learn why God often placed Egypt as a land of protection for Israel.

The Bible has an internal history as well as an external one. The Dickson Bible provides us with some of the most critical information which we need and which is readily available in a certain section at the end of each book of the Bible.

God has blessed us with Bible study for many years. In all these years, with many editions of the Bible available to us, the Dickson King James Bible has provided us with the most easily accessible information about the internal history of the Bible itself. It unifies His Story in all its Providential aspects.

One of the most important distinctions of Principle Approach learning is that we discover the unity of all subjects as they relate to the Westward Course of the Gospel. America could not be established until her settlers were Biblically prepared. In fact, Miss Hall included a memorable Election Sermon in her volume *The Christian History of the American Revolution: Consider and Ponder*. Reverend Foljambe speaking of America, states on page 47b:

"Not until the tenth century was it discovered by the Scandinavians, and only then to be hidden away again until the time should be ripe for its settlement, by a people providentially prepared for its occupancy."

America's Christian History depends upon Biblical principles of character, government, and education. The Principle Approach is dedicated to teaching Biblical principles and relating them to "The Hand of God in American History." With the Dickson Bible we can enjoy binding Biblical history as a chain of events bringing all things together for His Story.

# References

## for "The Christian Idea of the Child"

Bruce, A. B., *The Training of the Twelve*. (Bruce) New York: Armstrong and Son, 1908.

Ellicott, John Charles, D.D., *An Old Testament Commentary for English Readers*. (Ellicott, O.T., Vol. _) London: Cassell & Company, 1887.

Hall, Verna M., *The Christian History of the American Revolution: Consider and Ponder* (*Consider & Ponder*). San Francisco: Foundation for American Christian Education, 1975.

Hall, Verna M., *The Christian History of the Constitution of the United States of America*, Vol. I: *Christian Self-Government*. (CHOC) San Francisco: Foundation for American Christian Education, 1960. Articles cited: "The Rise of the Republic of the United States," by Richard Frothingham (1890), pages 283–359; quoting Samuel Adams, page XIV; "The Footprints of Time," by Charles Bancroft (1879), pages 5–9.

Henry, Matthew, *Commentary on the Whole Bible*. (Henry)

MacDonald, George, *Creation in Christ*. (MacDonald) Wheaton, Illinois: Harold Shaw Publishers, 1976.

Scudder, Horace E., *Childhood in Literature and Art: With Some Observations on Literature for Children*. (Scudder) Boston: Houghton, Mifflin and Company, The Riverside Press, Cambridge, 1894.

Slater, Rosalie J., *The Family and the Nation: Biblical Childhood*. (*Biblical Childhood*) San Francisco: Foundation for American Christian Education, 2002.

Slater, Rosalie J., *Teaching and Learning America's Christian History: The Principle Approach*. (T & L) San Francisco: Foundation for American Christian Education, 1965.

Webster, Noah, *American Dictionary of the English Language*, Facsimile 1828 Edition (Webster, 1828). San Francisco: Foundation for American Christian Education, 1967.

Scriptures are from the King James Version, except where noted.

# THE CHRISTIAN IDEA OF THE CHILD

## by Carole G. Adams

As a ten-year-old, John Quincy Adams was the typical Massachusetts farm boy, carrying mail regularly from Boston to Braintree, reading Smollett and Rollins, and studying French and Latin poetry. John, his father, was away tending the nation's business and confidently left John Quincy to serve as his mother's best hand on the family farm. This represented quite a responsibility for a young boy, especially considering a war was about to commence nearly within earshot. A letter written at this age to his father presents a clear profile of John Quincy's character and his literacy:

Dear Sir,

I love to receive letters very well, much better than I love to write them. I make but a poor figure at composition; my head is much too fickle. My thoughts are running after birds'-eggs, play and trifles, till I get vexed with myself. Mamma has a troublesome task to keep me steady, and I own I am ashamed of myself. I have but just entered the third volume of Smollett, though I had designed to have got half through it by this time. I have determined this week to be more diligent, as Mr. Thaxter will be absent at court, and I can not pursue my other studies. I have set myself a stint, and determine to read the third volume half out. If I can but keep my resolution I will write again at the end of the week, and give a better account of myself. I wish, sir, you would give me some instructions with regard to my time, and advise me how to proportion my studies and my play, in writing, and I will keep them by me and endeavor to follow them. I am, dear sir, with a present determination of growing better,

Yours,
John Quincy Adams

P.S.— Sir, if you will be so good as to favor me with a blank-book I will transcribe the most remarkable occurrences I meet with in my reading, which will serve to fix them upon my mind. (Hall, *Consider & Ponder*, p. 605–06)

A quick look at John Quincy's letter compels us to contrast the ten-year-old child of 1777 with those in our churches, our neighborhoods, and in our own homes today. It proposes the question: "What happened in 225 years in our culture to change so dramatically the expectations of the character and literacy of our children?"

In the eye of societal expectations in John Quincy's generation he was not exceptional; today's societal view of the child by contrast labels both his character and literacy level exceptional indeed. The years across which we view John Quincy show us also the slow erosion of the Christian idea of man and government in our nation, decade by decade, to be ultimately replaced by an inferior, one-dimensional, and secular view of man. The present predicament we face reveals that for American children, expectations are small and there is little true vision. Overall, we as a nation fail to agree with God about our children. They must be 'protected,' pandered, indulged, even worshipped, and definitely sold short. The time is late, but the mandate remains for American Christians to step up to the noble and exalted Biblical virtues of parenthood and education needed for our children to reach the fullest expression of their value in Christ. It is essential to the generation of children we currently rear and educate that we study to know the answer to the question, *What is the Christian idea of the child?*

## JESUS AND THE CHILD

Jesus himself who made some surprising remarks about children demonstrated the Christian idea of the child. He shocked his own disciples. The most tender scenes in the Gospels involve children: Jesus healing children, or welcoming children to himself, or holding up a little child to teach his disciples about God, or exhorting Peter on the beach at Tiberius, in a parting scene, to *"Feed my lambs."* He taught us that grownups have to learn again the child-like connection to the father-heart of God, and by so doing be filled with hope and faith.

"Brothers, have you found our king? There He is, kissing little children and saying they are like God. . . .

"The God who is ever uttering Himself in the changeful profusions of nature; . . . who never needs to be, and never is, in haste; who welcomes the simplest thoughts of truth or beauty as the return for seed He has sown; . . . the God of music, of painting, of building, the Lord of Hosts, the God of mountains and oceans; . . . the God of history working in time unto Christianity; this God is the God of little children, and He alone can be perfectly abandonedly simple and devoted. . . ." (MacDonald, page 34)

Observe the bringing of little children to Jesus in Mark 10:13–16:

*"And they brought young children to him, that he should touch them: and his disciples rebuked those that brought them. But when Jesus saw it, he was much displeased, and said unto them, Suffer the little children to come unto me, and forbid them not: for of such is the kingdom of God. Verily I say unto you, Whosoever shall not receive the kingdom of God as a little child, he shall not enter therein. And he took them up in his arms, put his hands upon them, and blessed them."*

Here we have the contrast of the 'human' and the 'divine' in dealing with children. The disciples discounted the importance of the bringing of the children to Christ. Jesus quickly and emphatically ". . . took it very ill that his disciples should keep them off; *When he saw it he was much displeased.* 'What do you mean? Will you hinder me from doing good, from doing good to the rising generation, to the lambs of the flock?'. . . He ordered that they should be *brought to him,* and nothing said or done to hinder them; suffer *little children,* as soon as they are capable, to *come to me,* to offer up their supplications to me, and to receive instructions from me. . . . He came to set up the *king-*

132

*dom of God* among men, and took this occasion to declare that that kingdom admitted *little children* to be the subjects of it, and gave them a title to the privileges of subjects. Nay, the kingdom of God is to be kept up by such: they must be taken in when they are little children, that they may be secured for hereafter, to bear up the name of Christ. . . . He received the children, and gave them what was desired; . . . out-did the desires of these parents; they begged he would touch them, but he did more. . . . He *took them in his arms*. . . . If we in a right manner bring our children . . . to the arms of his pity and grace, . . . He *put his hands upon them*, denoting the bestowing of his Spirit upon them . . . and his setting them apart for himself. . . ." (Henry, Vol. V, page 517)

Observe the place of children in the Kingdom in Matthew 18:1–6:

*"At the same time came the disciples unto Jesus, saying, Who is the greatest in the kingdom of heaven? And Jesus called a little child unto him, and set him in the midst of them, And said, Verily I say unto you, Except ye be converted and become as little children, ye shall not enter into the kingdom of heaven. Whosoever therefore shall humble himself as this little child, the same is greatest in the kingdom of heaven. And whoso shall receive one such little child in my name receiveth me. But whoso shall offend one of these little ones which believe in me, it were better for him that a millstone were hanged about his neck, and that he were drowned in the depth of the sea."*

In *The Training of the Twelve*, A. B. Bruce says, "What children are unconsciously, that Jesus requires His disciples to be voluntarily and deliberately." We are to study to be childlike. ". . . Childlikeness such as He exhibited is an invariable characteristic of spiritual advancement, even as its absence is the mark of moral littleness. . . . The great ones in the kingdom, . . . throw themselves with such unreservedness into the work to which they are called, that they have neither time nor inclination to inquire what place they shall obtain in this world or the next." (Bruce, pages 202–203)

Matthew Henry (Vol. V, page 252) says, "Grown men, and great men, should not disdain the company of little children, or think it below them to take notice of them." The emphasis here is on receiving children, and not offending them.

Jesus "proceeded to enforce the warning by drawing aside the veil, and showing them a momentary glimpse of that very celestial kingdom in which they are all so desirous to have prominence. 'Lo, there! see those angels standing before the throne of God—these be ministering spirits to the little ones! And lo, here am I, the Son of God, come all the way from heaven to save them! And behold how the face of the Father in heaven smiles on the angels and on me because we take such loving interest in them!'" (Bruce, p. 206)

"The attitude which Christ took toward children must contain the explanation of the attitude which Christianity takes toward the same, for the literature and art of Christendom become the exponents of the conception had of the Christ." Horace Scudder, author of *Childhood in Literature and Art*, 1894, a scholar interested in the views of childhood represented in various periods of history, makes these eloquent observations about "the general aspect which childhood wore to Jesus Christ. . . .

"The eyes of this Jesus, the Saviour of men, were ever upon the new heavens and the new earth. The kingdom of heaven was the burden of his announcement; *the new life which was to come to men shone most plainly in the persons of young children*. Not only were the babes whom he saw and blessed to partake of the first entrance into the kingdom of the spirit, but *childhood possessed in his sight the potency of the new world*; it was under the protection of a father and mother; it was fearless and trusting; it was unconscious of self; it lived and did not think about living. The words of prophets and psalmists had again and again found in the throes of a woman in labor a symbol of the struggle of humanity for a new generation. By a bold and profound figure it was said of the great central person of humanity: 'He shall see of the travail of his soul and be satisfied.' A foregleam of that satisfaction is found in his face as he gazes upon the children who are brought to him. There is sorrow as he gazes upon the world, and his face is set toward Jerusalem; there is a calm joy as he places a child before him and sees in his young innocence the promise of the kingdom of heaven; there is triumph in his voice as he rebukes the men who would fain shut the mouths of the shouting children that run before him. The pregnant words which Jesus Christ used regarding childhood, the new birth, and the kingdom of heaven become indicative of the great movements in life and literature and art from that day to this. The successive gestations of history have their tokens in some specific regard of childhood." (Scudder, pages 50–52, *italics added*.)

The twenty-first century is an age in opposition to the Christian view of the child. The general view of childhood in our society is hostile to the values our Lord Jesus Christ established. This is an age perishing, though *"God so loved the world, he sent his only begotten son, that whosoever believeth in him shall* not *perish, but have everlasting life."* The word *perish* means also *waste*—that whosoever believeth in him shall *not be wasted*. Our children are our progeny, our stewardship. In American society and education today, waste is a reality, one that we must eliminate if we are

to obey God in rearing and educating His children. We must reassert the Christian idea of the child in our philosophy of family, education, government, and life. We must take our cue from the model of Biblical child growth and development found in Luke 1:80 and Luke 2:40: *"And the child grew, and waxed strong in spirit. . . ."* *"And the child grew and* [became] *strong in spirit, filled with wisdom: and the grace of God was upon Him."* Nurturing a strong spirit in our children means taking seriously the admonition implied by II Timothy 3:15 giving our children a knowledge of *"the holy scriptures, which are able to make* [them] *wise unto salvation through faith which is in Christ Jesus."* Of equal importance, it means relating to our children on the basis of God's Principle of Individuality, honoring the unique reflection of God's image within. *"By faith Moses' parents hid him for three months after he was born, because they saw he was no ordinary child, and they were not afraid of the king's edict."* (Hebrews 11:23, NIV, *emphasis added*.) Likewise we must see our children as unique— there are no "ordinary" children, only specially created ones, with a purpose, a calling, all their own.

How does this Christian idea of the child contrast with the views of childhood in other periods of history?

## CHILDHOOD: PAGAN AND CHRISTIAN VIEWS

In *The Christian History of the Constitution of the United States of America: Christian Self-Government,* the Christian and pagan ideas of man are identified in the writing of Richard Frothingham's "The Rise of the Republic of the United States," 1890 (Hall, CHOC, Vol. I, pages 1–2, *italics added*):

. . . Christianity—the basis of the good, permanent, and progressive in modern civilization—first appeared in the world. At that time, social order rested on the assumed natural inequality of men. The individual was regarded as of *value only* as he formed a part of the political fabric, and was able to contribute to its uses, as though it were the end of his being to aggrandize the State. This was the pagan idea of man. The wisest philosophers of antiquity could not rise above it. Its influence imbued the pagan world. The State regarded as of paramount importance, not the man, but the citizen whose physical and intellectual forces it absorbed. If this tended to foster lofty civic virtues and splendid individual culture in the classes whom the State selected as the recipients of its favors, it bore hard on those whom the State virtually ignored,—on laboring men, mechanics, the poor, captives in war, slaves, and women. This low view of man was exerting its full influence when Rome was at the height of its power and glory. . . .

This low view of man translated into a low view of the child—a pagan view. Horace Scudder notices that in Greek and Roman literature, ". . . there is scarcely a child's voice to be heard in the whole range of Greek poetic art. The conception is universally of the child, not as acting, far less as speaking, but as a passive member of the social order. It is not its individual life so much as its related life which is contemplated." (Scudder, page 21)

Frothingham's voice rises dramatically here as he announces the most revolutionary change in the history of the world—the event that changed the condition of man and child for all time!

". . . Christianity came with its central doctrine, that man was created in the Divine image, and destined for immortality; pronouncing, that, in the eye of God, all men are equal. This asserted for the individual [and for the child] an independent value. . . ." This principle is seen in Jesus' treatment of children in the Gospels.

Frothingham continues, "It occasioned the great inference, that man is superior to the State, which ought to be fashioned for his use. This was the advent of a new spirit and a new power in the world." (Hall, CHOC, page 2) And Christianity was also the advent of a new day for education.

## AMERICAN CHRISTIAN EDUCATION

This Christian idea of man and government gave rise eventually to the first expression of Christian civil government embodied in the constitutional republic of the United States of America. Our duty as American Christian educators therefore has a particular quality. Samuel Adams gave the rallying cry: "Let divines and philosophers, statesmen and patriots, unite their endeavors to renovate the age, by impressing the minds of men with the *importance of educating their little boys and girls,* of inculcating in the minds of youth the fear and love of the Deity and universal philanthropy, and, in subordination to these great principles, the love of their country; *of instructing them in the art of self-government,* without which they never can act a wise part in the government of societies, great

or small; in short, of leading them in the study and practice of the exalted virtues of the Christian system. . . . " (Hall, CHOC, p. XIV, *emphasis added.*)

As American Christians, our accountability includes the trust God gave us in our liberty—to use it for His glory, to honor Him in its practice. We must instruct our children in the art of self-government. We must ennoble our children ". . . by a sense of [their] own dignity through the practice of a system of self-government which improves the condition and promotes the interest of each while it produces harm to none." (Bancroft, in CHOC, p. 8) In God's providence, we have a peculiar calling among nations—a holy priesthood that includes *both* the propagation of the Gospel and the keeping of the torch of Christian civil liberty for all.

## BIBLICAL CHILDHOOD

In her study of Biblical childhood, Rosalie Slater observes that, in the Hebrew home, ". . . [t]he spiritual nature of the household was built upon deeply reli-

gious principles and customs of worship which permeated every act, every day, every week, and every month of the year." (*Biblical Childhood,* page 75) Central in the

Hebrew home was the observance of providential events in the history of Israel in which the children took part.

"As the children asked, the father in each family would relate, in language which a young child could understand, the 'whole national history of Israel, from the calling of Abraham down to the deliverance from Egypt and the giving of the law.' The more fully this account was given and the better it was explained, the greater impression it made upon the memory of each child present. So from the time of babyhood were the young of each new generation made aware of the details of their unique history of liberty." (*Biblical Childhood*, p. 77) The Hebrew home that nurtured our Lord in his childhood shared this focus of remembering the mighty acts of God in history.

The nurturing Hebrew home has affected history extraordinarily. The story of Samuel, the prophet-priest-judge, exemplifies Biblical childhood and its effect on the life of a nation. Samuel faced the very conditions of spiritual decline and calamity that we face in America today by giving an answer that is a challenge to every Christian leader of this generation. To appreciate the full impact and inspiration of this account, read Miss Slater's Biblical research using the Ellicott *Commentary for English Readers* (1887) in her *The Family and the Nation: Biblical Childhood*. Because Samuel learned to hear and obey God at a young age, he became an instrument of reform in his nation.

Samuel's ministry to the homes of Israel convinced him that the educational level of the nation had plunged during its years of failed leadership from the priesthood. "In his long wanderings up and down among the people, during his toil in the course of his vast labour of religious restoration, he had seen how deep was the ignorance of the children of Israel. In the troublous days of the judges the arts, music, poetry, and history were unknown. The chosen race cared for none of these things.

'To remedy this state of things, Samuel founded the schools of the prophets, in order that, by their agency, the mental condition of the people, might be raised, and men trained to serve God in Church and State. . . .

'The instruction was essentially free, open to all comers, and, when educated, the prophet might return to his farm, or to some occupation connected with city life. But he was from henceforth an educated man: and he had been taught, too, the nature of Jehovah: how He was to be worshipped, and what was the life which every member of a covenant nation ought to lead.

'Thus Samuel's schools not only raised Israel to a higher mental level, but were the great means of maintaining the worship of Jehovah among the people. . . . But the prophetic order had in Samuel's mind another important function. It was to be a permanent public power alongside the priesthood which already existed, and of the kingly office, which he, Samuel, had inaugurated. It was intended especially to offer to the latter, when inclining to tyranny, a powerful opposition, founded on the Divine Word. Throughout the history of Israel we find the prophetical order not merely the preachers of a high and pure morality, and a lofty, spiritual religion, but we see in them . . . the protectors of the oppressed subjects against the despotic monarch, the steady defenders of the down-trodden poor against the exacting and covetous rich.

'In one sense, they filled the position which the priesthood ought to have occupied, had the representatives of that order done their duty, but who—as Samuel well knew, not only from the past said history of the period of the judges, but from his own personal observation at Shiloh during the life-time of Eli—had been tried, and had been found miserably wanting.'

Thus, Samuel's great work began with *revival, repentance,* and *restoration*—and it began in the families of the nation. It was a direct outcome of his own family life and preparation that sprang from the prayers of his mother, Hannah, and the faithfulness of his father, Elkanah. Samuel's first work, too, with the Schools of the Prophets allowed the nation to build back the ability to become a GOD-REMEMBERING people. It allowed for Israel to once again produce its national identity as a "peculiar people" chosen of the Lord for a special contribution to the world. Out of the Schools of the Prophets came forth:

*National poets*—extolling once more for open hearts the mercies of the Lord and his great goodness to Israel.

*Annalists*—or historians, recounting the many providential events in God's blessing to the nation.

*Preachers of Patriotism*—invoking remembrance of Israel as a special nation.

*Moral Teachers*—leading them back to the great rock of Mosaic morality, bursting forth into a cleansing stream of individual and national reformation.

*Exponents of the Law*—dealing with the detail of obedience as set forth in the Ten Commandments.

*Pastors*—comforting with the "staff and rod" these sheep of the Great Shepherd.

*Politicians*—preaching the polity of God's jurisdiction and government of man and the universe, and of Israel's direct rule by God.

'But their most essential characteristic,' states Ellicott of the graduates of Samuel's Schools of the Prophets was 'that they were instruments of revealing God's will to man.'

(Ellicott in *Biblical Childhood*, pages 44–45)

## THE CHRISTIAN IDEA OF THE CHILD MANDATES A DISTINCT METHOD OF EDUCATION

The Christian idea of the child mandates a new wineskin of education that is distinctly Biblical. Parents and teachers of the present generation were educated in a system of humanistic, secular education and its atheistic, evolutionary view of man and of the child. Much of modern Christian education, in schools and home schools, attempts to coat the secular philosophy, method, and curriculum with scripture, prayer, and Christian doctrine, or with a lavish slather of classical content. What is needed is a whole new form—a new form that is thoroughly Biblical, restoring the true heritage of American Christian education.

Where does this exist? What does it look like? How

does it work? It is the original philosophy of education, the product of the reformation, existing in the colonial and founding eras of our nation, that produced the character and intellects of our founding fathers. The research that identifies it today for our children was published by the Foundation for American Christian Education in 1965 in Rosalie J. Slater's *Teaching and Learning America's Christian History: The Principle Approach.* It is "America's method of Biblical reasoning that makes the Word of God the heart of every subject in the curriculum." It is practiced in schools and home schools across the country and in many other countries.

The Principle Approach aims at forming Christian

character in the student. It has been shown measurably to produce a Biblical worldview in the student's thinking. Measured by the Nehemiah Institute annually since 1985, Principle Approach students out score all other Christian students given this same test. Therefore the results meet education's whole purpose: forming character, forming Biblical reasoning, and producing outstanding scholastic results.

Principle Approach education methods are distinctively governed by Biblical principles and include both content mastery and the satisfaction of the real needs of children. A visit to a Principle Approach classroom reveals a teaching and learning dynamic that presupposes the value of the individual child who bears the image of God. There is an elevation of spirit and an appreciation of learning and reasoning. The teacher is the living textbook, and the students become the producers of their own learning, as they are inspired, cultivated, consecrated, and instructed towards the fullest expression of their individual value in Christ.

Education as defined in his 1828 *Dictionary* by the father of American Christian education, Noah Webster, is "all that series of instruction and discipline which is intended to enlighten the understanding, correct the temper, form the manners and habits of youth, and fit them for usefulness in their future stations." To this definition Webster adds a small sermon for our benefit: "To give children a good education in manners, arts and science, is important; to give them a religious education is indispensable; and an immense responsibility rests on parents and guardians who neglect these duties." The word 'religious,' in Webster's

day, meant the practice of Biblical Christianity in every area of life and character. In education this requires more than spreading a Christian vocabulary over the old wineskin of progressive education. It requires the restructuring of education, creating a new wineskin: the identification and application of Biblical principles in every subject and as a yardstick for choice of methods used. "*And no one puts new wine into old wineskins; otherwise the new wine will burst the skins, and it will be spilled out, and the skins will be ruined.*" (Luke 5:37)

While it is not the purpose of this article to expound the Principle Approach method, it is essential to suggest that modern, 'progressive' education, whether in public, private, or home schools, does not qualify as an acceptable mode of educating our children if we indeed propound a Christian idea of the child. Such methods of education can be described generally as 'content-centered' or 'child-centered.' Content-centered education methods are governed by curriculum objectives—covering the material. Teaching is often rote and objective; curriculum is piecemeal, presenting facts in blocks, bits, blobs, and blurs; instruction is norm-directed, skill-targeted, test-motivated. Materials are often consumable, fill-in-the-blank workbooks. The 'needs' and interests of the child, on the other hand, govern child-centered education methods. Teaching is often passive, allowing discovery and expression full reign, resulting often in the 'uncorrected' temper.

Children educated from a child-centered method are gratified sensorially and temperamentally, but they are not satisfied in heart and character.

## THE CHRISTIAN IDEA OF THE CHILD
## REDEFINES THE ROLE OF TEACHER AND PARENT

The "Child," a "progeny of parents," is, according to Webster: "One weak in knowledge, experience, judgment or attainments; One young in grace, . . . humble and docile." Parents have charge of children and are accountable as stewards. Teachers are those who ac-

cept a professional role of educating the progeny of a community as entrusted by parents. As Christian teachers and parents, we must define our roles according to Biblical principles and according to our place and purpose in His Story. We must examine ourselves and discover how much of the past conditioning to false values we still retain in dealing with the precious children God entrusts to us. To teach Christianly is to examine the Master Teacher and learn from him. Jesus taught by modeling and is the archetype of teaching, the standard, the ideal. Through his Son, God answered the question of what teaching is. Jesus taught by loving, accepting, affirming, receiving. He taught by healing, by enabling, by prodding. He imparted truth in such a way that its intrinsic beauty delighted his students, captivated their hearts and minds, so much so that two-thousand years later, our hearts are touched by his words and respond to his message. Every subject in the curriculum holds truth which, when captured and imparted by an inspired teacher, inculcates the love of truth and beauty. The teacher/scholar's love of the subject and love of the child is the "living textbook."

Jesus touched individuals, causing each person to feel especially loved. Teaching is in essence a relationship between the teacher and the student through a subject. Jesus related to each individual through His subject, salvation, by observing and satisfying the needs of those who came to him. We should not confuse the meaning of the word satisfaction with the meaning of the word gratification. To satisfy is to supply fully what is necessary and demanded by natural laws. To gratify is to give pleasure to, to indulge, as to gratify the senses, the desires, the mind, etc. Jesus satisfied the real needs of individuals so that they went away fully supplied. As teachers and parents, we must learn to identify the real needs of our children and satisfy them.

What are the real needs of children? The primary need is spiritual—to be born into the kingdom of God. Jesus satisfied the primary spiritual needs as caringly and surely as he met the physical needs of those he encountered. Teachers and parents follow suit, making the spiritual the priority, and following Jesus to meet the further needs:

1. Significance: Children need to have a deep sense of safety, of feeling loved, cherished, and significant.

2. Trust: They must develop trust in the character of the key adults in their lives.

3. Acceptance: Children must acquire an adequate self-value, based upon their acceptance of their own individuality as a gift from God. Adult treatment of the child communicates unmistakably of his worth and potential.

4. Purpose: If children see themselves as having a place in history and see the events in their lives in light of a providential God, then they can have assurance for their present and future.

5. Work: They need activities that are real to them, significant, intriguing, not just amusing or entertaining—ennobling work or occupation—in order to acquire vision for the value of their life and purpose.

6. Wisdom: Children need wise guidance from adults to help them make sense of their experiences and interpret their world through principles.

7. Models of Christian self-government: Children need Christ-governed adult models who accept the authority that is theirs by virtue of their greater experience, knowledge, and wisdom, and who represent God's government in their lives.

8. Models of Christian character: Children need adult models who exemplify personal qualities of victorious Christian character, who are productive and committed, and who inspire them.

The attitudes Jesus expressed in His dealings with individuals should be our attitudes with children. His respect for each person's worth should inspire us to display deep and genuine appreciation for the individuality of each child. He was genuine, spending time and giving unfeigned attention to individuals on a human level, making himself accessible. Jesus made his teaching concrete, giving his students tangible truth and presenting the most abstract message that ever existed in the most easily understood and concrete words.

He readily confronted discrepancies between verbal conviction and life reality, detecting and communicating in a mentoring style to bring each individual to his fullest expression.

As teachers, the Principle Approach methods and curriculum, and philosophy of education, allow us the liberty and creative expression to satisfy the real needs of our students in a whole way. We see each child as an individual of infinite value, made in the image of God and worthy of our respect. We see children full, ready to be cultivated, inspired, consecrated, and instructed rather than seeing them as empty, fit only to be stimulated, motivated, enculturated, or indoctrinated. We see the tutorial needs of students, that each one as an individual is entitled to his own learning style and instruction, that every child can be elevated to a worthy standard. We see that our students need to produce, not consume only—expressing themselves in the arts, music, drama, and athletics, developing every talent, exercising their whole potential.

Because we know that truth satisfies, we identify Biblical truth in every subject, giving our children the bread of life as a steady diet, not just crumbs and morsels. We show them the whole of God's purpose for man in history so that they can place themselves securely in the kingdom of God, sure of where they stand, able to accept their position on the chain of Christianity, and envision the purpose of their personal lives.

Suffer the little children to come unto me, and forbid them not:
for of such is the kingdom of God.
And he took them up in his arms, put his hands upon them,
and blessed them.

Mark 10:14–16

May our children be likewise blessed, that they may lead their generation to Christ, and that He might be glorified.